Day Trips with a Splash
Swimming Holes of California

by Pancho Doll

Running Water Publications
San Diego, California

Read this

Hiking is a potentially dangerous activity. Some sites in this book are reached via unmaintained trails or by overland travel where no trail may be present. As such, they require skill and strength beyond normal requirements for safe hiking. Although the book tries to point out potential dangers, conditions may change on the trail as well as in the water. River levels fluctuate widely during the year. Seasonal indicators are meant as guidelines, not as guarantees of when a place may be safe for swimming. People regularly drown or are seriously injured because they overestimate their abilities or exercise otherwise poor judgement. Rocks in rivers may be steep and slippery. Be cautious and aware even when walking casually in a river or creek bed. Jumping into water from rocks is inherently dangerous. You are responsible for locating submerged obstacles that could cause injury.

The overwhelming majority of swimming holes featured here are entirely on public land. A few cross, or lie near private land that, when visited for this book, did not appear to be posted or were marked with signs giving the public limited permission to use the property. In all events, you must obey no trespassing signs.

Library of Congress Cataloguing-in-Publication Data
Doll, Pancho
Day Trips with a Splash: The Swimming Holes of California
Includes Index.
1. Hiking—California—Guide-books.
2. Trails—California—Guide-books.
ISBN 0-9657686-4-3   LCCN 97-067213

First Edition	June 1997	**Revised Edition**	July 2003
2nd print	March 1998	2nd print	June 2006
3rd print	November 2000		
4th print	June 2002		

Acknowledgments

Thanks to my many friends and family for their support and encouragement, among them Rodney Bosch, Lauren Dodge and Andrew LePage. Special thanks go out to Vic Pappalardo who, during a trip to the South Yuba River, initiated the idea of a swimming hole guide and to Paul Harton, for help in the Motherlode. Thanks also to Jill Mahanna for editing. Red pen never looked so good. And finally, a deep genuflection to Sean Haffey for invaluable advice on graphics and layout and to Steven Greenwald for financial input. Thank you all.

The Running Water Staff

Photographer   **Duncan Freely**

Designer   **Ngo Tan Ligne**

Diving Consultant   **Flip Obermore**

Spiritual Advisor   **Rev. Bob Tism**

To my mom for being ever willing to load us
kids in the car and take us to the river.

You could tell by the dent of the heel and the sole
They was lots o' fun on hand at the old swimmin'-hole

— James Whitcomb Riley (1849-1916)

Contents

Humboldt, Mendocino & the Redwoods

Shasta-Trinity

Chico, Paradise & the Feather River

The Motherlode

Yosemite Park & the Central Sierra

The Seqouias

Santa Barbara & Ojai

The San Gabriel & San Bernardino Mountains

Santa Ana & Laguna Mountains

Introduction

There's a story in my family. It's about me and a pair of purple swimming trunks. They were bought at Target, made of polyester and knit tight to stay snug on an 8-year old's skinny hips. And stay they did. For one entire summer, Memorial Day through Labor Day, those purple trunks were my sole undergarment. To the best of my, or anyone else's recollection, I never took them off.

And why should I? Our family spent part of nearly every day on the small Ozark river that bordered our farm. In the morning we fished; in the evening we barbecued and in the hours between no tadpole was safe. Whether skipping stones, diving off logs or doing spectacular parabolic exits from a rope swing, wet was the only way to stay during humid Midwestern summers. A boy had to be committed to his swim shorts.

It was natural to start exploring creeks and canyons when I moved to California, and explore is the right word. Traveling up wild waterways often produced startling discoveries. In contrast to the mountain vistas most people associate with hiking, swimming holes are physical enclosures. When you hike up a mountain the peak is nearly always visible, but swimming holes sneak up on you. Turn a corner and you discover some glorious piece of liquid jade surrounded by alders.

The arcade of trees that so often tops rock walls lends a feeling of privacy. It's the outdoors' indoors and perhaps why stories of love recurred so often when I asked people for swimming hole anecdotes. Mountain panoramas turn a mind outward while the enclosing comfort of a canyon turns thoughts inward. Rather than stretch out your arms you want to wrap them around something.

Oddly enough, it's not the water that makes a swimming hole great; it's the rock. The best ones have an architectural quality. Southern California has superb sandstone bowls built like a Roman forum. There are dark metamorphic pools in the Mendocino National Forest that have the feel of a private bath house. The Sierras have classic granite holes containing so many water-worn shapes, it's like walking through a garden of abstract sculpture.

Locating the swimming holes featured in *Day Trips with a Splash* wasn't always as much fun as it might sound. I left a cozy apartment on the beach and a cushy job as a staff writer for the *Los Angeles Times* to spend nine months on the road, covering California from Oregon to San Diego County. I put 25,000 miles on my truck, thrashed two pairs of sport sandals, one GPS and ate more Powerbars than anyone should have to.

I also met an awful lot of people having fun. It left me with the impression that most guide books are too reverent. A weekend outdoors can be a spiritual experience without sounding like a trip to church. It's supposed to be fun. Swimming holes are *fun.* The sun starts getting hot, the laundry comes off, and instead of quoting John Muir you're doing cannonballs into a cauldron of emerald water.

I'd even argue that swimming holes are *the* most complete trip to the mountains. Hiking alone isn't. There is always space between the hiker and the trees, always a separation between us and the ground we travel over. But water touches every part of the body with the perfect contact of immersion. People form attachments to these places. Several times I met parents and children at a swimming hole that the parents themselves had been coming to since childhood.

Beyond fun, there's a metaphor here. Think of the stream as the work week, all noise and repeated motion. The swimming hole is the weekend, a place where the pace slackens, the issue gets broader and the water grows quiet enough to show a reflection. Follow the maps and see for yourself.

Using this guide

The convention in outdoor guide books is to take a small area and detail *every* trail in it. This book takes a region and, using swimming holes as a theme, tells readers the *best* places to go. Beyond a unique subject matter, *Day Trips with a Splash* is laid out in a new, easy-to-use format. One page is a USGS topographic map with directions and latitude/longitude coordinates for those with global positioning system (GPS) receivers. The facing page has a picture of the swimming hole along with the review and icons detailing key information about the spot.

I tried to include a range of difficulties in each chapter, some accessible enough to take small children, others remote and with a high expectation of privacy. But first, a few terms need to be outlined in a quick and dirty glossary so you know what you're getting into.

> *Moderate scrambling* means you might bash a knee or skin an elbow and your friends may laugh at you.
>
> *Third-class scrambling* means that if you fall, it will hurt. You may receive injuries and your friends might have to help you back to the car. You may even need medical help.
>
> *Bushwacking* is considered light if you can do it in shorts. It's moderate if you wish you had pants on. It's heavy if you wish you had pants and boots.
>
> *Basins* are broad and shallow, usually less than four feet deep. Little or no sense of enclosure.
>
> *Pools* are deeper, between six and eight feet deep with proportionately less surface area than basins.
>
> *Tubs* have an even smaller surface area, usually room for only a couple of people. They're five to seven feet deep with near complete enclosure and are most often associated with waterfalls.

Holes are generally the same proportion as a pool but deeper and with a tighter enclosure. If you can dive into it, it's a hole.

The Approach

The right-most icon tells how long or difficult the hike is. Most people are familiar with the symbols ski areas use to evaluate the difficulty of the slopes. Here they are redefined for hiking.

 Beginner Less than one-half hour. No more than a couple of tricky steps. You can bring kids.

 Intermediate Up to one hour. May include moderate scrambling, boulder hopping, bush-whacking or amphibious hiking. You feel like a kid.

 Advanced Longer and/or steeper approach. May include extensive boulder hopping, deep river fords or 3rd class scrambling with potentially injurious fall. Leave the kids at home.

 Expert Three-hour approaches over difficult terrain or technical approaches requiring rope. No kidding around.

The Season

The set of icons to the left of the approach icons tell you which season is best for each swimming hole. If you only want to enjoy the beauty of a spot, swimming holes are pretty much year-round attractions. However if you're amphibious by nature, you've got to consider the season before you jump in. Remember, conditions vary and there's no reliable way to look at a calendar and judge when a river is safe. People drown every year because they get into major rivers too early in the season when the water is too high. Don't swim in any body of water unless it's absolutely still or running very slowly. Here's the test: toss a tree branch in at the top of the pool. If the branch goes over the falls or out the rapids downstream before you can get your clothes off, the water is too fast.

Spring Smaller or dryer watersheds. The spring swimming holes open as soon as the water's warm enough (April or so) and end when the water gets stagnant. The closing varies greatly, but the Fourth of July is a good benchmark. Just about all of Southern California is a spring thing.

 Summer Fourth of July through Labor Day. Usually streams and creeks between 1,500 and 4,000 feet elevation. Tributaries to major Sierra rivers and sometimes the rivers themselves depending on how heavy the snow pack is. Some are better earlier in the summer, some later. If the hole has both a spring and a summer designation that means late June through July is best.

 Fall As late as October at lower elevations. Some steep, narrow swimming holes on smaller streams may receive a fall designation because water is too fast even during the moderate summer flow. A summer and a fall combination (the main stems or major forks of Sierra rivers) means water may still be too high in early July and you might have to wait until later in the month. Given that they drain elevations as high as 10,000 feet, the water stays cold well into the summer, but you can probably use it on hot autumn days through September.

The Company

The next group contains four icons which generally let you know who or what you can bring for companionship and who you're likely to find.

 Kids You're generally safe bringing little dippers of any age to a swimming hole with a beginner's approach. However, short approach holes without a child icon indicates either the rocks are too steep or the water is otherwise inappropriate for junior. On an intermediate approach, a child under seven may tire.

Dogs Many dog owners have difficulty finding places to take their canine pals, what with restrictions on dogs in wilderness areas and national parks. The "Bowser" icon indicates spots in national forests where you don't *have* to keep the dog on a leash and where he's not going to run into lots of other hikers and disturb them.

 The Boom Box Brigades Crowds likely. Potentially rowdy. Likely to be evidence of at least one broken beer bottle.

 The Butt indicates one of two things. Either there's a chance you will find skinny dippers (most places in the Motherlode, for instance) or the place is private enough that you and your companion(s) can opt for no tan lines.

Overall rating

The left-most icon is the overall rating. There are about a dozen points on which to judge the quality of a particular spot. The Holy Trinity is height, depth and privacy. Tall, vertical rock gives a sense of enclosure above the waterline and often produces a fat deep end. All entries in this book are at least six feet deep. The ratings are fair, good, excellent and classic.

To get an excellent rating they must have some compelling vertical feature like a fall or a jumping rock. A swimming hole may not be rated classic and also have a boom box designation.

The privacy assessment is based on what you'd expect to find during a peak weekend. Most of the spots are far enough up canyon that if you do meet other people, they're apt to be like-minded outdoors enthusiasts who will enhance the experience rather than detract from it.

Doubtful means one dozen or more people in the area. Bring a bag to pick up trash other people leave behind.

Possible indicates fewer than six people likely. Consider going elsewhere on weekends.

Likely suggests the most you would expect to find is one other group.

Guaranteed says little evidence of visitorship other than a slight trail. If somebody else arrives at the swimming hole, you're probably being followed.

Usability

Usability is the collection of features that make a swimming hole comfortable for humans. It's difficult to take full enjoyment of a spot if it's too steep to sit down. Bare rock and blazing sun can shorten a day, too.

Seating A well-shaded sand beach is best. Low angle slabs can be very comfortable, especially if the rock has smooth declivities worn in it by the water. These depressions are called *buckets* if they're just big enough for only one to sit in. Seating for two or more is called a *bench seat*. A slab is considered flat if a can rolls slowly enough that you can catch it before it hits the water. It's sloping if you can't set the can upright without it tipping over. The slab is considered steep if there's a danger you yourself might tip over. Boulders are less comfortable than slabs. Typically they're more jagged and many are too small to lie on at all. For the purposes of this book, boulders are considered small if they're the size of a trunk. Medium boulders are the size of a car. Large boulders are the size of a cabin and massive boulders are the size of a house.

Sun and shade On what part of the swimming hole will the sun be shining from mid-afternoon on and is there a place you can go to escape it.

Entry and Exit There are more than a few swimming holes you can jump in only to realize there's no easy way back out.

Temperature Water in the mid 60 to 70 degrees is considered just about ideal.

Jumps Basically how high. Where possible I've tried to explain what the bottom features are like. Talk to locals if they're available for safety information, but most importantly get in the water and have a look around for yourself.

You are responsible for your own safety. Anyone jumping from cliffs should not depend solely on this guide for safety information.

Aesthetics

This is another qualitative category describing the water and the shape of the rock enclosure.

Water quality Mainly the clarity and color of the water, whether gin clear, Coke-bottle green, emerald, jade, turquoise or tea. What's the visibility and does it have much plant glop. Points are deducted if there's a dam upstream. Human pollution is largely irrelevant since nearly all the spots are on national forest land and well above any settlement, although range cattle lower water quality in a few places.

Geometric sides are either generally round or with coherent angles such that the waterline forms a recognizable shape like a rectangle or circle. The bottom is even, containing small cobbles, sand or smooth stone.

Wavy enclosures signify that straight lines or curves, when found, are not sustained. Submerged rocks and boulders may obscure the bottom contour.

Jagged swimming holes have no discernible lines to the rock structure. Not necessarily a bad thing. An apparent imperfection can become an attractive feature such as when large boulders poke through the surface to create platforms for diving or lounging.

The Maps

Material for the map pages was scanned from United States Geological Survey 7.5-minute topographic maps. In all but a few cases the elevation contours are 40 feet. Every effort was made to get the most current maps; however, trails are often not shown and some other information may be out of date. Although it's difficult to get completely lost following a stream or river, it's a good idea to bring a compass on long trips and be proficient in its use.

Where helpful, latitude and longitude annotations were added. Coordinates were checked against physical maps using the WGS 84 map datum. Pinpoint accuracy is what the GPS promises and usually delivers. Still, the possibility for error is significant, both in the operation of individual navigation units and in generating coordinates published here. The coordinates and the map location represent a best effort to locate the swimming hole being reviewed, but neither are guaranteed to be completely accurate.

Computer users can get electronic copies of the maps. Send in proof of purchase from the back of the book along with a copy of the store reciept to become a registered user of our web site then download the maps to print out at home, much more elegant than taking the entire book into the hills when you only need two pages.

Finally, it's recommended that you use a forest service recreation map for highway information and for information on campgrounds if you want to make a car camping weekend of it.

Tactics and Ethics

Most of the approaches are best done in trail running shoes. Sports sandals are acceptable for the shorter and intermediate ones. Only a few require boots. Remember, he who is shod lightest travels fastest.

The simple fact you're holding this book identifies you as a person of distinction and judgment. You're probably aware of low-impact outdoor ethics, don't cut switchbacks, that sort of stuff. Nevertheless, here are a couple things day users should keep in mind.

When hiking off trail don't skid down steep slopes. Rather, place your foot carefully and weight it gingerly so as not to dislodge dirt and rocks. A stealthy tread prevents erosion and avoids twisted ankles. In some cases where there is a steep descent or a stream crossing, it's an excellent idea to bring a ski pole or some sort of sturdy walking stick. When walking on or near the stream, it's best to step on the tops of exposed rocks where possible. Avoid sloshing through shallow gravel and the stream margins. Lots of critters lay their eggs there and you can do a devil of a lot of damage with one footstep.

Don't urinate within 200 feet of open water.

If you want to be a good steward of the outdoors, also bring an empty plastic bag big enough to hold a couple of beer cans or whatever other small bits of trash you may encounter.

Careless users are a big reason people complain that including a spot in a guide book ruins it because too many people show up. My response is that it's a big state and I should sell so many books. Still, I did find a handful of places that are either ecologically sensitive or genuinely pristine and I had serious reservations about letting every lite beer drinker in the country know about them.

The solution was to publish those places separately in a limited distribution booklet called *The Splash Pro Tour*. It's available for a nominal fee to members of the Sierra Club, Friends of the River, Nature Conservancy, local volunteer groups…any organization in which membership demonstrates a degree of outdoor citizenship. That serves to protect the resource while encouraging people to become active in environmental groups and rewarding those who already are. Wild places need a constituency if they are to remain protected.

Humboldt, Mendocino & the Redwoods

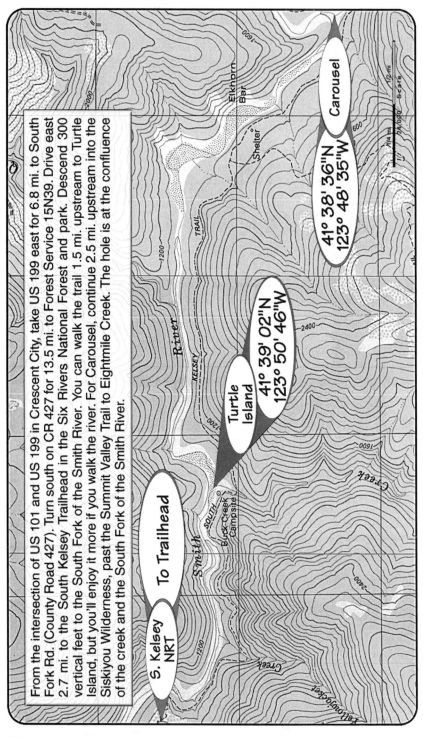

From the intersection of US 101 and US 199 in Crescent City, take US 199 east for 6.8 mi. to South Fork Rd. (County Road 427). Turn south on CR 427 for 13.5 mi. to Forest Service 15N39. Drive east 2.7 mi. to the South Kelsey Trailhead in the Six Rivers National Forest and park. Descend 300 vertical feet to the South Fork of the Smith River. You can walk the trail 1.5 mi. upstream to Turtle Island, but you'll enjoy it more if you walk the river. For Carousel, continue 2.5 mi. upstream into the Siskiyou Wilderness, past the Summit Valley Trail to Eightmile Creek. The hole is at the confluence of the creek and the South Fork of the Smith River.

Carousel

Everybody says the Smith River is a great place to swim. True, but the largest undammed white water river in the state does have some limitations. Hwy 199 intrudes on much of the middle fork producing crowds with beer coolers and boom boxes and the north fork is a devil of a long drive from just about anywhere. That pretty much leaves the south fork for day trips on the Smith. Carousel is about 35 feet around and that's just the deep end. From shore to shore the pool is a broad, flat 80 feet, which is to say not much of a vertical description. Entertainment comes in the form of an eddy where the main current of the Smith carries a swimmer 20 or so feet downstream to where a creek enters and cycles you back up and into the main current. Idle amusement, yes. But people reportedly spend large parts of a lazy afternoon rotating in a slow circle, looking at the sky.

Expectation of privacy is good, however a fire ring indicates some usership. A mountain bike is a good approach tool, although it's a burly, burly ride back up. Be aware that a small part of the trail lies within the Siskiyou Wilderness and mountain bikes are prohibited. There's no sign marking the wilderness boundary, but it's shortly after Buck Creek. Personally, I wouldn't consider it a crime against man and nature to ride all the way to Carousel, but it *is* against the regs.

Tish Tang

Turtle Island

Water so clear that if you dropped a shiny quarter ten feet to the bottom, you'd still be able to read the mint date. The serpentine rock that lines the Smith is very hard, producing little sediment, thus giving the river its crystal clear reputation. An overlay of pillow basalt gives the water its beautiful color. The Smith also holds the distinction of being the largest wild and scenic river in the nation as well as being the only river in California that is completely free flowing from its tributaries to its discharge.

Dazzling water quality boosts what would otherwise be a fair hole to good. The hole has a couple of six-foot jumps with nice ledges on the near bank for entering and exiting the water. The shores are jagged and uneven, as opposed to smooth contours that would make this swimming hole more geometrically appealing. A large turtle-shaped rock in the center of the river makes a nice place to sun. The water is cold—in the low 60s—and even on a hot day you have to take a deep breath before jumping in. The expectation of privacy is fair. Since it's right along a trail, you're likely to see one or two groups passing by.

Bonus Feature: What looks like an undeveloped climbing boulder is next door to the swimming hole. It's about 20 feet tall with a heinous overhang. It needs extensive cleaning, though.

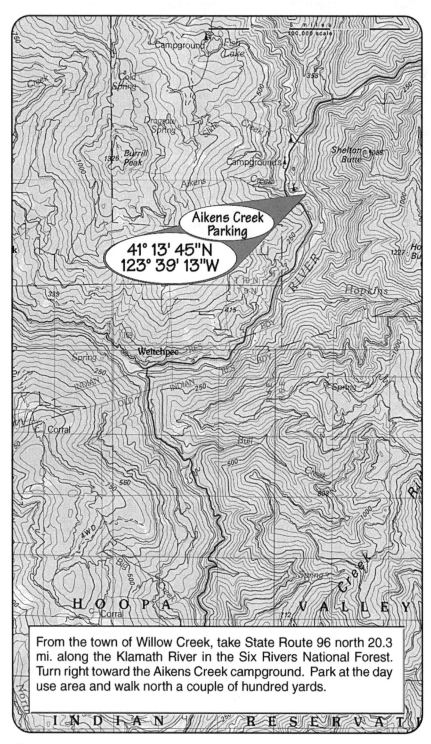

Aikens Creek
Parking

41° 13' 45"N
123° 39' 13"W

From the town of Willow Creek, take State Route 96 north 20.3 mi. along the Klamath River in the Six Rivers National Forest. Turn right toward the Aikens Creek campground. Park at the day use area and walk north a couple of hundred yards.

Aiken's Creek

The Klamath River at Aiken's Creek is typical of major waterways in the Six Rivers National Forest. An elbow in the river causes the water to excavate the opposing wall which, when river levels drop, turns into a cove with a slackwater pool. The river turns and broadens into a shallow basin then picks up velocity and spills over a rapid. It seems to be a pattern repeated over and over on rivers in the Coast Range, most frequently on the Klamath.

Here at Aiken's, the cove extends 80 feet back from the main current. Ledges are eight to twelve feet high; the water is at least as deep. You regain the ledges after a dive by walking out the back of the cove and up some slabs to the left. The ledges are crumbly and not at all comfortable. Absolutely no adjoining beach. The day use parking area is the only place to spread out a picnic.

Walking between the swimming hole and the day use area on a really hot day you may hear popping coming from the bushes growing in a level area of mixed soil and gravel. They're redbuds that have pods which evidently burst in hot weather as a method of disbursing seeds. It's a little like standing in a bowl of rice crispies.

Expectation of privacy is poor. The river is only a couple hundred yards from the highway and Aiken's Creek Campground is next door. Seating is limited. Shade is hard to find, also.

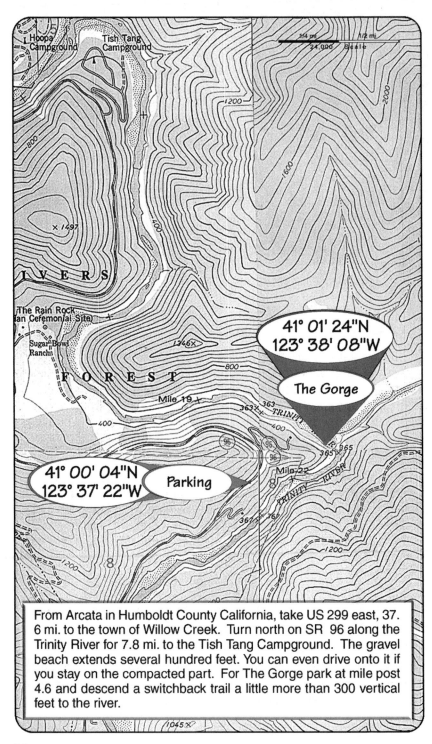

From Arcata in Humboldt County California, take US 299 east, 37. 6 mi. to the town of Willow Creek. Turn north on SR 96 along the Trinity River for 7.8 mi. to the Tish Tang Campground. The gravel beach extends several hundred feet. You can even drive onto it if you stay on the compacted part. For The Gorge park at mile post 4.6 and descend a switchback trail a little more than 300 vertical feet to the river.

Tish Tang

Fully conjugated the name is Tish Tang a Tang, a corruption of the Hupa Indian phrase "land that sticks out into the water." The swimmable part stretches almost one half mile and is wide, flat and featureless except for Prayer Rock, a 25-foot outcrop that it's said Native Americans used for ceremonies.

Tish Tang doesn't belong in a hiking guide except that it's got a cool name and it's a good spot for families with small children. Generations of automobiles have compacted the cobbles and sand into a roadway that even low-clearance, two-wheel drive cars can make it out onto. It's so easy to reach the river that an elderly gentleman said he brought his wife to soak in the reputedly healing waters less than two weeks after she broke her hip.

The river has degenerated some from its status as a spiritual and restorative waterway. Bob Braxton, a commercial fisherman from Trinidad said he's snorkeled much of the river here, including a deep, deep hole under a madrone tree about 200 yards downstream from Prayer Rock.

"I find lots of beer cans, that's for sure. People on float trips, they toss the cans over and lots of them get caught in that hole," Braxton said. "At one time or another I've found virtually every domestic and most of the imports."

Trinity River

The Gorge

Enough water to conduct naval maneuvers. It's at a sharp elbow in the Trinity River where the prime swimming area is 50 feet wide and stretches more than 350 yards around the north to west bend. There are three rock outcrops that unfortunately don't give off into deep water the way rocks at Tish Tang do. There is, however, a good jumping rock on the opposite shore at the top of the bend. Be careful swimming over to it because the water is deceptively swift.

Plenty of beach, most of it east-facing. By 10 a.m. the sand is already scorching. The main beach is a 200-foot arc of fine sand that occupies as much as 30 feet between the water and the rock walls. Because the beach curves along with the river, you have a little more privacy since you can always find a place around the corner. The rock outcrops create partitions that further divide the beaches and produce a swimming hole that can absorb lots of people.

Good thing too. On a holiday weekend I saw 20 cars parked at the turnout. Must be a respectful crowd because when I visited on the day after the long weekend, I didn't find a single piece of litter.

9.25 mi from Hwy 299

Todd Ranch Access

40° 48' 10"N 123° 33' 25"W

Lunch Bucket

11.5 mi from Hwy 299

Surprise Creek

From the town of Willow Creek, take State Route 299 south into the Six Rivers National Forest for 4.25 mi. to Forest Service road 447 (South Fork Road). Drive 9.25 mi. south to the Todd Ranch Access. Park & walk 200 yds to the river, ford to the west and continue upstream 50 yds to a long, flat terrace. Walk .25 mi. south to where the terrace ends and splash 20 yds upstream to the pool. For Surprise Creek continue on South Fork Rd another 2.2 mi. to the road's end where the creek joins the South Fork Trinity River. There's also a good swimming hole at the confluence of Coon Creek and the river. The trail is 200 yds uphill from the parking.

Lunch Bucket

This must be a tough neighborhood if you're a fish. Eagles, otters and ospreys compete for food and lodging along this slow, deep channel. The basin is around 60 feet wide and about 100 yards long. It has a couple of modest sandbars where the expectation of privacy is excellent. Solitude is bolstered because a couple of undistinguished pools at the bottom of the access trail divert most bathers. You may be interrupted by the occasional paddler, although most kayaking and rafting takes place on the main stem of the Trinity River rather than the south fork. The otter living here *will* come by for a look, though.

The pool is only rated as good because it lacks a vertical feature like a falls or a jump. The approach is interesting, though. Moderate bushwhacking and a river ford lead to a delightful walk along a terrace that's flat as a griddle and lightly forested. No understory of plants to become tangled in, just mature conifers and one *immense* oak whose canopy is big as a circus tent. Getting to the terrace is easy if you don't mind swimming. But if you have items you need to keep dry, the ford is a little more tricky. Best advice is once you reach the bottom of the access trail, bushwhack 30 or so yards upstream through an infernal tangle of willows. Water there should be only waist deep during the summer. A walking stick is an invaluable aid on crossings like this.

Granite Creek (Pro Tour)

Surprise Creek

Plenty of river to play in. A low ridge forces a huge turn comprised of four 90-degree zigzags. The last 30 feet of Surprise Creek falls into the South Fork of the Trinity at one of these bends creating a chest-deep pool that's really nice when the falls are pumping. Of course the pool is plenty deep when the river level is up, and that's usually when the falls are more forceful. But by the time the river is at swimmable levels, the fall is diminished, though still attractive. About 50 yards downstream from the fall is a minor rapid, but upstream you can swim 250 yards and more through flat water. Immediately to the left of the fall is a stone beach with pebbles rather than the cobbles ,which make the typical Trinity River beach uncomfortable. What's more, there's a small sand beach just above the rock one and it's lined with alders so you can enjoy that rarest of luxuries on the Trinity—natural shade.

All in all, a good hole and the ridge gives a nice sense of depth to the canyon. But with only a ten-minute approach, the expectation of privacy is poor. Better travel a few minutes by trail farther upstream to Coon Creek primitive camp if you need to be alone. There, a long flat portion of river connects with the holes around Surprise Creek, but it's a piece of water that's up above one of the aforementioned zigzags. As such it's much more private. You might see one other group here on a weekend.

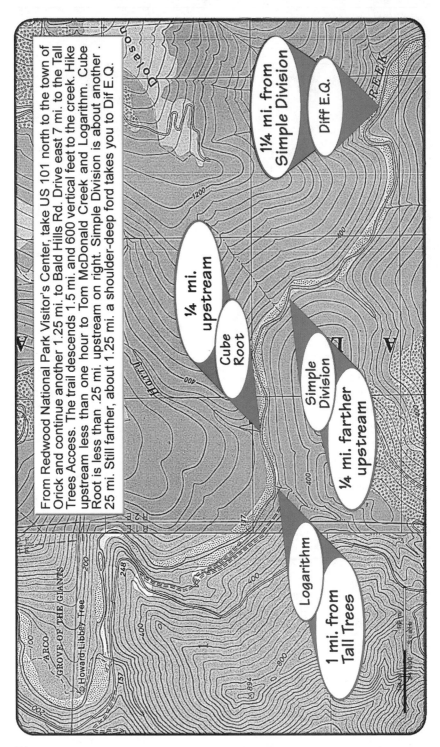

From Redwood National Park Visitor's Center, take US 101 north to the town of Orick and continue another 1.25 mi. to Bald Hills Rd. Drive east 7 mi. to the Tall Trees Access. The trail descends 1.5 mi. and 600 vertical feet to the creek. Hike upstream less than one hour to Tom McDonald Creek and Logarithm. Cube Root is less than .25 mi. upstream on right. Simple Division is about another .25 mi. Still farther, about 1.25 mi. a shoulder-deep ford takes you to Dif E.Q.

1¼ mi. from Simple Division

Diff E.Q.

¼ mi. upstream

Cube Root

Simple Division

¼ mi. farther upstream

Logarithm

1 mi. from Tall Trees

Logarithm

A redwood trunk lodged at a small elbow in the creek creates an *incredible* diving board, fifteen feet long, six feet high and pointed downstream into the heart of the Redwood National Park. The hole is only about five feet wide directly under the trunk, but it broadens into a shallow pool that stretches 100 feet farther downstream. Walk in the shallows at the top of the pool and you'll probably notice that your right foot gets much colder than your left. An adjoining creek empties much cooler water into Redwood Creek and it takes several yards for the two streams to mix completely. Also, polliwogs thrive in the shallows.

The trail to Redwood Creek passes by what's officially the world's tallest tree. Unofficially the champ lost its title several years ago when weather destroyed much of the canopy. Park officials say one of the other trees in the grove probably holds the title now, but no official honors have been conferred yet.

Check this swimming hole out while it lasts. It's hard to tell how long this log has been lodged on top of the rocks or how long it's likely to stay put. Even if seasonal rain washes the diving log downstream, there are plenty of more stable swimming holes upstream.

Mineral Bath (Pro Tour)

Cube Root

So dark and mossy, you feel a fern might pop up between your toes. The shade comes from a mature redwood growing above a triple-lobed rock wall on the right side of the pool. When the water is low, there's a perfect little beach on the left side. Lie on the narrow crescent of sand, tilted as it is toward the water, and your eyes point directly at the redwood's trunk just as straight and rigid as a deacon on Sunday. The tree crowns the center rock while its roots reach around the stone like it's holding on for life.

It is. Redwoods lack a central taproot and are easily toppled by erosion. You'll find many trunks scattered along the shore and they often produce features that add texture to the river. A trunk lodged across the current may form a dam that creates a small pool. Trunks that lodge parallel to the flow may produce an artificial bank that preserves some trees still standing near the shore, but rarely do redwoods survive close enough to the creek to actually shade a swimming hole. That's a big part of what makes Cube Root so special.

Sadly, the wall isn't *really* a diving ledge. The water will be no more than six feet deep if the creek level is low enough to create a nice beach. The cracks you'd have to climb are too wide to use your hands, too narrow to wedge your body inside. Still, to look at the tree perched there 25 feet above water, it's tempting.

Seven Falls (Pro Tour)

Simple Division

Honey, I'm home. A horseshoe-shaped rock splits the river in two and creates a little pool that's shaped like a miniature coral atoll. A tree trunk has tipped right into the middle of the pool, creating the mother of all sunning logs. The outer edge of the horseshoe offers a low dive into a pool that's smaller but deeper than the one inside the horseshoe. The beguiling feature is the hue of the water, a gray-green slate color that I haven't seen in any other river in the state. It's probably a function of the blue schist that's common on the creek. Look for the enchanting color where the gravel is clear of moss or algae and the water is less than three feet deep.

Water is part of what makes Redwood Creek the best approach in this book. Of course an approach that passes the tallest tree in the world scores big points, but the wet hike through the warm, clear water and a flat creek bed make this the most pleasant splash up a river you could imagine. An amazing proportion of the stones are flat, smooth and the perfect size for skipping. I'm certain that if rock skipping becomes an Olympic sport, this is where Team America will train. Kids go ape here, not just for the skipping rocks, but because polliwogs abound.

Rattlesnake Creek

Diff E.Q.

A series of three boulder holes. The lowest is a gorgeous channel of water bordered by a terrific beach with plenty of places to stand or sit on the main boulder. You might be able to jump from the main rock, however getting to the top of it will require some agility, courage and commitment. Water is ten to twelve feet deep. The upper holes are deeper and set within a tangle of water-worn rock that looks like a sculpture gallery. Most notable is a sofa-sized piece of rock with as many as 100 different water grooves carved in it. There's such a complex set of motion implied in the grooves that the differential equation describing it would weigh more than the rock itself.

Excellent expectation of privacy since it's a bit of a walk. Some folks make it an overnight trip. Remember, regulations and wilderness ethics mandate camping at least 200 feet from open water. Bury human waste and pack out everything else. The sand beach is a tempting site, but ecologically unwise to camp on. Can be noisy also.

David Titzler of Simi Valley was repeatedly awakened by river otters. Apparently otters aren't great stalkers. A pair of them was trying to sneak up on his food cache, but each time they got close the animals came unglued and started chattering with excitement.

"They kept me up all night," he said.

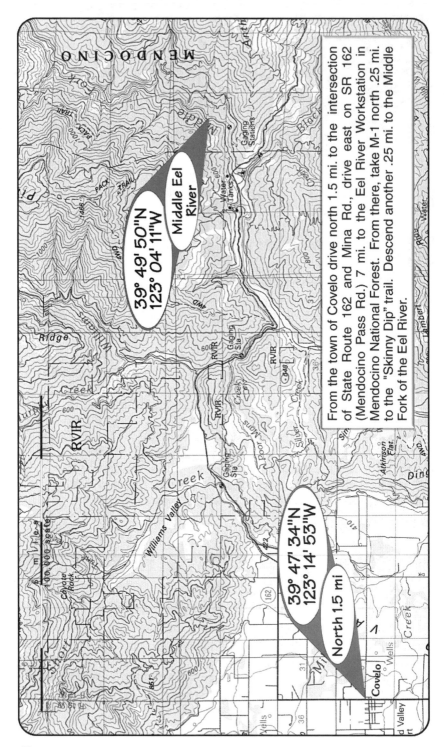

From the town of Covelo drive north 1.5 mi. to the intersection of State Route 162 and Mina Rd., drive east on SR 162 (Mendocino Pass Rd.) 7 mi. to the Eel River Workstation in Mendocino National Forest. From there, take M-1 north .25 mi. to the "Skinny Dip" trail. Descend another .25 mi. to the Middle Fork of the Eel River.

39° 49' 50"N
123° 04' 11"W

Middle Eel River

39° 47' 34"N
123° 14' 53"W

North 1.5 mi

The Falls

Effluvia, flotsam, dirt and detritus. The Coast Range's rapid rate of erosion means the Middle Eel carries the heaviest bedload of any river in the world except the Yantgze. In the Coast Range it seems that any bit of water that tumbles far enough to make a splash is designated "a falls." I'm not sure what they're calling the falls here. The main pool faces southwest on a flat, open channel just below a small cascade. (The falls?) The pool is 80 to 100 feet long, 10 to 12 feet deep and ringed with big boulders that give it a nice round look. The bottom has cobbles and boulders with a fair amount of sand. You might want to go exploring some of the holes and pools above the falls. Not a lot of jumps here, but bring goggles or a dive mask because there are a couple small underwater grottos and surge holes that are fun too explore.

Incidently, on the gravel bars you'll find quite a bit a driftwood which fuels many campfires. Visitors however appear to be very responsible. Campfires rings are set on open gravel and have nothing but ashes in them, no half burned trash or broken glass bottles. So when the water comes up, it all gets washed away. Parking can be tight on a weekend when you might expect to find a dozen or more people. The walk is short enough that you can bring a folding chair or baby *accoutrements*.

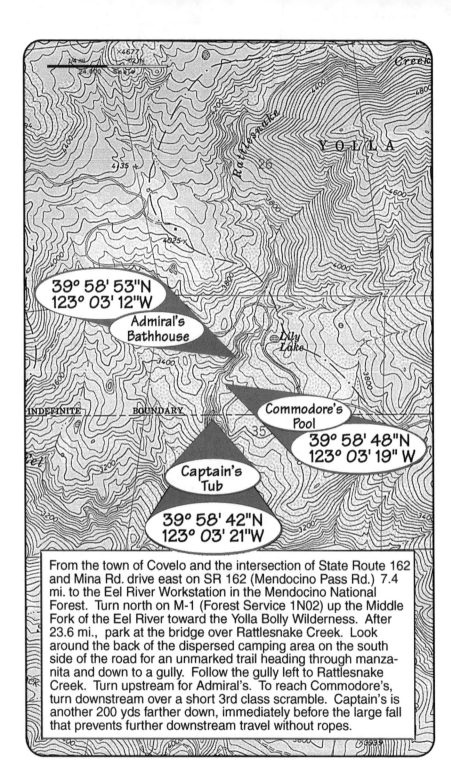

39° 58' 53"N
123° 03' 12"W

Admiral's Bathhouse

Commodore's Pool

39° 58' 48"N
123° 03' 19" W

Captain's Tub

39° 58' 42"N
123° 03' 21"W

From the town of Covelo and the intersection of State Route 162 and Mina Rd. drive east on SR 162 (Mendocino Pass Rd.) 7.4 mi. to the Eel River Workstation in the Mendocino National Forest. Turn north on M-1 (Forest Service 1N02) up the Middle Fork of the Eel River toward the Yolla Bolly Wilderness. After 23.6 mi., park at the bridge over Rattlesnake Creek. Look around the back of the dispersed camping area on the south side of the road for an unmarked trail heading through manzanita and down to a gully. Follow the gully left to Rattlesnake Creek. Turn upstream for Admiral's. To reach Commodore's, turn downstream over a short 3rd class scramble. Captain's is another 200 yds farther down, immediately before the large fall that prevents further downstream travel without ropes.

Commodore's Pool

A funnel-shaped pool with a seven-foot falls. The most remarkable feature is the series of ledges that march down into the pool like a short set of stairs. And if you don't favor the gradual method of immersion, you can jump in off the adjoining rocks. Water is little more than seven feet deep, so be prepared to touch bottom. The temperature on Rattlesnake Creek is on the chill side, low 60s in July.

The most characteristic feature of Rattlesnake Creek is the rock forming the creek bed. It's a dark chert inlaid with fine seams of white quartz that run pencil-thin and straight as a razor for yards. Most veins are set at consistent angles to one another, creating an endless series of quadrangles and trapezoids inlaid in the dark stone. The rock has the texture of 000 emery paper. Incredible traction even when wet. Because it's so dark, it does get mighty hot. Consider bringing something to sit on. Also, don't confuse the beguiling lines of quartz with the white streaks that local members of the avian community deposit. Water ouzels apparently find the dining pretty good along Rattlesnake Creek.

In sum, very pretty though not overwhelming. Be prepared for a short third class scramble some 200 yards above Commodore's. The expectation of privacy appears excellent to guaranteed.

Admiral's
Bathhouse

Admiral's Bathhouse

A secret garden surrounded by a sun-blasted forest. Most of the summer is broiling. But down in the bottom of this tiny, precious gorge it's cool and green. More than one dozen water-loving plants grow from every nook and cranny in a place that's got more than its share of nooks and crannies. A 20-foot fall empties into a sharply defined, funnel shaped hole with a moderately steep ledge on the right that comfortably seats two people. Opposite the ledge, sheer rock rises almost 100 feet to a slim, 70-foot-wide strip of sky at the top of the gorge. A dicey scramble from the ledge to the lip of the fall lets you rest in cool water while you gaze directly into the cauldron below.

A note on snake safety: Be on the lookout for rattlesnakes in the gully that descends to the gorge. It's rocky and brushy with plenty of ankle-high shade for buzz worms. Boots would be a good choice.

Although the gorge is where it's at, don't neglect a handsome no-approach hole just above the bridge. Privacy is doubtful except on weekdays. The bridge is only barely out of sight, shielded from view by a curtain of alders. Still, it's a nice place for young children. Check it out if you're bivouacked with the little dippers at the unofficial car camping spot across the road.

Stony Creek

Captain's Tub

More pools and potholes, deep shade and miniature waterslides. Captain's is a perfect rectangle. A short set of ledges leads into the pool on one side and a similar set of low stairs leads out the other side onto a sunning slab dappled with shade from an attending birch tree. The tub is no more than twenty feet long and six feet deep. Not the place to hold a fraternity rush party or a Labor Day picnic, but it's just fine for a couple. Notice the unusually large Indian bathtub just to the left of the fall lip as you face upstream. It's a perfect oval, 10 feet on the long axis and chest deep. It's left dry by receding water early in the season and since the container is small and easily heated, it's probably an outstanding place for an early inauguration of the swimming season.

On the way to the creek you may have noticed that the manzanita is enormous – trunks up to one foot in diameter and more. Native Americans pruned the bushes and raked the ground underneath to make harvesting the berries easier. The practice protected the scrub from fire, thus producing the unusually large specimens.

Check out the fall immediately below. It marks the limit of how far you can travel downstream without ropes. Then spend the rest of the summer exploring other parts of the creek. You'll put your sport sandals on and go running off like a kid at summer camp.

From the north shore of Clear Lake, begin at the intersection of State Route 20 and Main St. Drive north on Main .25 mi. to 2nd. A right left dogleg puts you on Middle Creek Rd. Drive northeast 40.4 mi. to Fouts Spring Rd. and bear left 2.5 mi. to the North Fork Cpg in the Snow Mountain Wilderness of the Mendocino National Forest. You can take the fisherman's trail up Stony Creek. A bench of land arcs 400 yds from northwest to northeast at 1,630 ft elevation. Just above that a major tributary comes in from the west and 10 minutes farther on is the overhang. Continue 15 minutes farther upstream for additional pools.

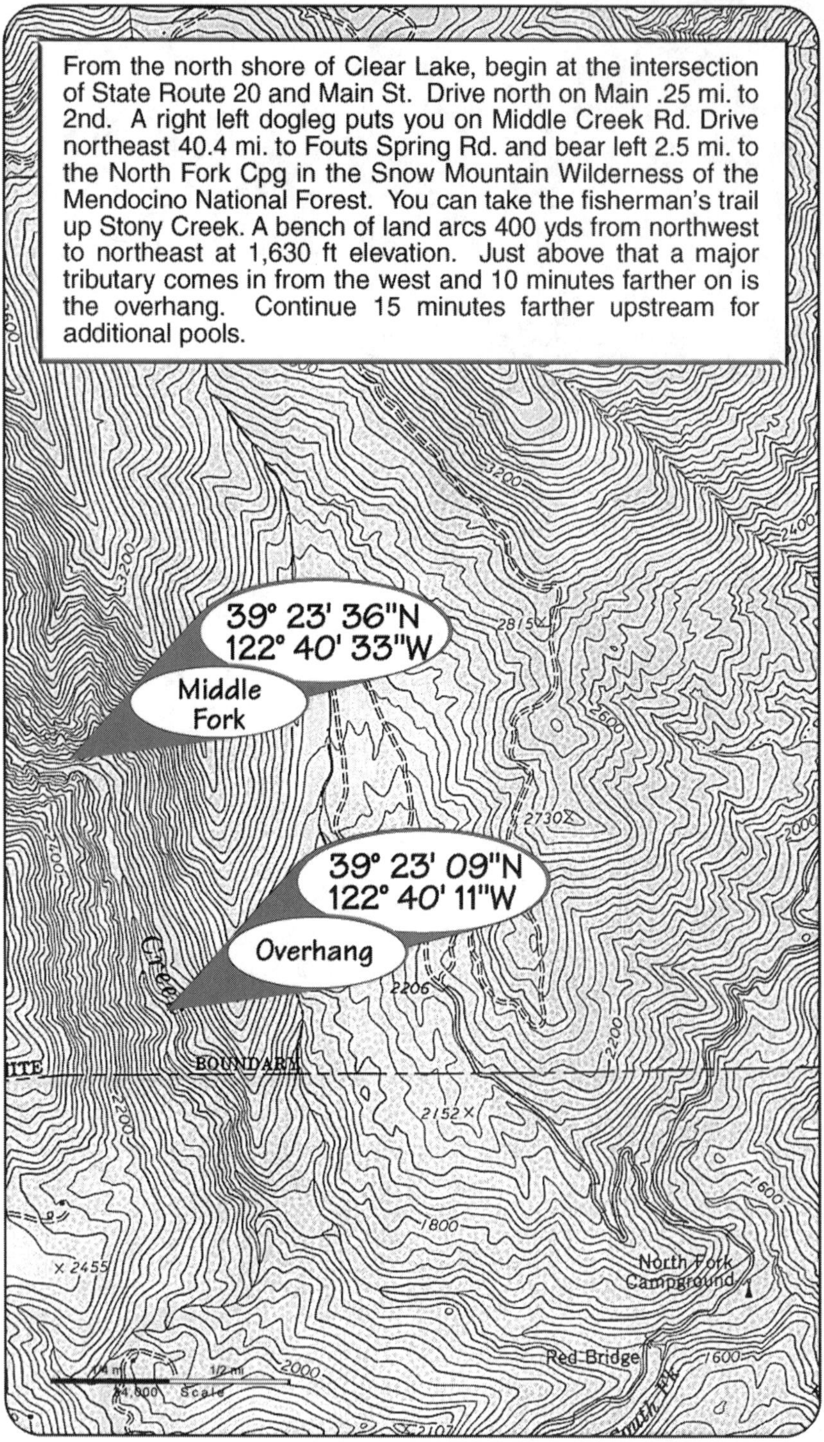

Stony Creek

Trout cold and Caribbean clear. A north-facing ridge sends the river down a narrow canyon that produces a couple of constriction falls about 125 yards apart. The upper one is churning and narrow. It's not going to wash you downstream and conk you on the head; You will get a pummeling, though. The water is magnificent—99 distinct shades of turquoise. It took all afternoon just to count them. Peer intently into the foam of the falls and you can see the water is really blue, the same electric hue produced by the phosphorescent algae that bloom in spring along Southern California beaches.

Down below the two falls is a third pool where the eye-catching feature is a deeply undercut band of rock. It produces an overhang that reaches eight feet over a modest pool. Not deep enough for diving, though. The seating, such as it is, you find on the north bank. Rocks are liberally coated with super slick brown algae. Tread carefully. Expectation of privacy is excellent.

Bonus Feature: Look for a wild fig tree downstream on the eastern bank. The tree has a couple of crops. The first is in early June. The second is in late July or early August. The grazing should be excellent. Just remember to leave some for the critters to eat.

Why Bother

Emerald Creek
Chest deep. If the place doesn't have at least one spot where you have to tread water, forget it.

Jed Smith
Waiouchi trail through Stout Grove. Gorgeous walk through the redwoods, but the opposite bank is strewn with RVs at Jed Smith park.

Swimmer's Delight
The VanDuzen passes through a fat stand of old growth timber, but it also goes through miles of dairy farms. Water quality is questionable at best.

Grays Falls
Fine for steelhead and salmon, but creatures without fins may find the water too fast. Also dam release water.

Sandy Bar
As many as 100 people on a holiday weekend. Pass.

High Rock
Bland. Too accessible.

Swinging Bridge
Pretty and fairly remote, but the water's only chest deep on a tall man.

Deadman's
Gross with litter. Dozens of cans, several socks and a disposable diaper.

Big River
Dirt bikes and target shooting, lots of timber company land. Muddy water.

Shasta-Trinity

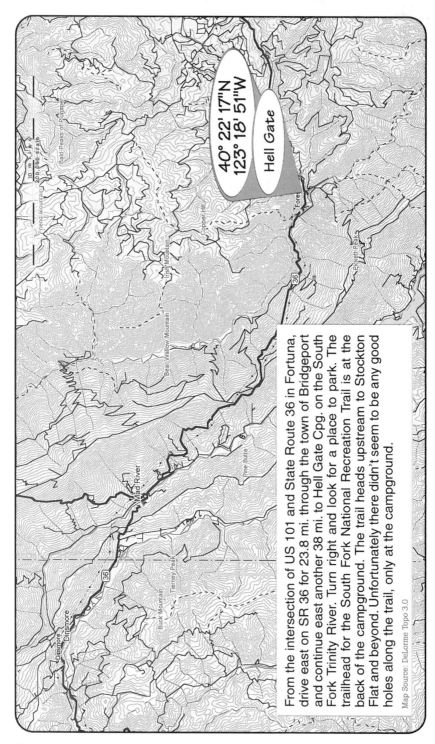

40° 22' 17"N
123° 18' 51"W

Hell Gate

From the intersection of US 101 and State Route 36 in Fortuna, drive east on SR 36 for 23.8 mi. through the town of Bridgeport and continue east another 38 mi. to Hell Gate Cpg. on the South Fork Trinity River. Turn right and look for a place to park. The trailhead for the South Fork National Recreation Trail is at the back of the campground. The trail heads upstream to Stockton Flat and beyond. Unfortunately there didn't seem to be any good holes along the trail, only at the campground.

Map Source: DeLorme Topo 3.0

Hell Gate

Highest Volvo coefficient of any swimming hole measured. Ford Explorers finished second and Subarus were third All of which is to say lots of families. Denesae McNicoll (pictured) is the third generation to ride the rope swing at Hell Gate. For 27 years without interruption the McNicoll family, their cousins, in-laws and even the in-laws' relations have spent their summers bobbing in the wide, slow water of the Trinity River's south fork. During the summer the river is sprinkled with air mattresses carrying people between the campground and the deep basins downstream. The most spectacular display is the evening when entire families raft together and sputter upstream on one giant vinyl lily pad.

A market may be developing for the popular lower campsites. A poll of vacationing families found they'd offer as much as $150 for a riverside camp if they found another car parked there. Along the campground the river itself is fair to good, more of a channel than an enclosed space. Zero expectation of privacy. Jumping rocks at the day use area downstream.

Bonus feature: *Beautiful* mountain bike rides on the South Fork Recreation Trail. It's an abandoned road studded with rocks and roots, making this a hot ticket for intermediate to advanced riders. Note: Riding across the bridge is expressly prohibited...don't get caught.

From the town of Willow Creek, drive south on State Route 299 for 9.5 mi. to Hawkins Bar. Turn north on Denny Rd for 29 mi. to Forest Service 7N15 in the Shasta-Trinity National Forest. Turn left and drive 5.6 mi north to the New River trailhead in the Trinity Alps Wilderness. Hike upstream 1.4 mi and, after crossing a nameless stream, look for a spur trail that leads to the creek, a broad bench of land, then a large gravel bar. Follow the river 100 yds downstream to the rock wall that is Grotto. The descent for Octopus is just under 2 mi from the trailhead. Look for the spur at the top of the second ridge after Grotto. Descend to the river and continue 150 yds downstream over cobbles, below a series of rapids.   Virgin Pool is easy. The trail leads right to the confluence of Virgin Creek and Slide Creek, entering from the right. Total 2.4 mi from the trailhead.

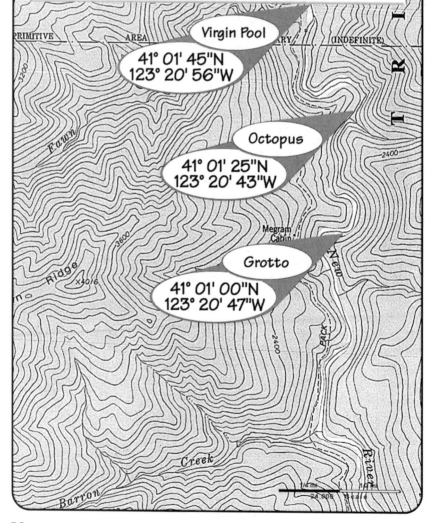

Virgin Pool
41° 01' 45"N
123° 20' 56"W

Octopus
41° 01' 25"N
123° 20' 43"W

Grotto
41° 01' 00"N
123° 20' 47"W

Grotto

Winner of the most *yin* award Here's a place that actually swallows light. A fern-covered rock wall rises like a scallop shell 30 feet above and six feet over a little jade-colored elbow in the river. The rock frames one side of a small pool that separates the cool grotto from a searing cobble beach on the other side. Absolutely no place to sit comfortably among the football-sized cobbles. You squat. The back of the grotto does have a slim ledge, barely deep enough to sit on and just wide enough for two people to perch there in the shade amid the deer ferns and shadows. It looks like an incredible place to kiss.

The pool itself is not too remarkable beyond the fact that it mediates so well between the two antagonists, light and shade. It's no more than seven feet deep and about fifteen feet in diameter. The river is not visible from the trail heading up canyon. There's a bench of land where people camp about 150 feet from the pool. This is where to drop your picnic basket since the beach is *really* uncomfortable. Expectation of privacy is good, although you can expect at least one group of hikers to visit during a weekend.

Octopus

Octopus

Barely a double diamond, but every inch a classic. Fast moving water squeezes through a five-foot notch in the rock before spilling into a deep, funnel-shaped pool bounded by vertical walls. Diving potential appears unlimited. On the near (left) side, ledge heights are seven, ten and twenty feet and they overhang the deepest part of a deep hole. Ledges on the far side range from seven to forty feet. Very difficult to reach the dive ledges on the right, though.

Getting down to the hole is a little tricky. The trail down is steep, although running shoes should suffice. Some minor bouldering moves and a wet landing if you lose it. There's a rope attached to a small madrone tree that you can use to let yourself onto a ledge that slopes into the hole, but for style points why not just jump in from the 20-footer.

You'll probably see mining claim papers posted on one of two mature ponderosas to the right immediately at the top of the trail spur. The mining claim itself is just above the hole and still appears to be patented, but doesn't appear to have been worked in some time. Expectation of privacy is excellent. The vertical description is brilliant, but the horizontal is weak. The beach is rocky and there's little shade, although you can duck into the alders at back of the gravel bar or nestle into a small patch of sand hard by the far wall. Mostly you grill.

Mossbrae

Virgin Pool

It's the definition of a wild river. No bridge crosses it and no road touches it. Water from Virgin Creek spills unmolested from the Trinity Alps into this tranquil pool that marks the beginning of the New River. There's nothing architectural about the headwaters. Nothing to jump from. Just a pool 70 feet in diameter, maybe 10 feet deep at the middle, beautifully round and fringed with Indian rhubarb and willows. More than anything it's a beautiful gathering of water. No beach, but there's a gravel bar with plenty of shade where some horsemen banged together a slapdash picnic table.

There was once much more—a forest service guard station, even a small store! Gold miners were legion in the Trinity Alps and New River lay at the head of a major pack route from Hoopa to the west. According to New River native Grover Ladd (1887-1972), the store was still there as late as 1888. Around 1940, long after the store disappeared, the Forest Service built a station. The station was rarely used by the time floods washed it away in 1964. Hikers and pack animals still cross here on their way into the high country. Compaction at the edge of the pool indicates lots of traffic.

Note: Steelhead making a comeback. Area closed to fishing.

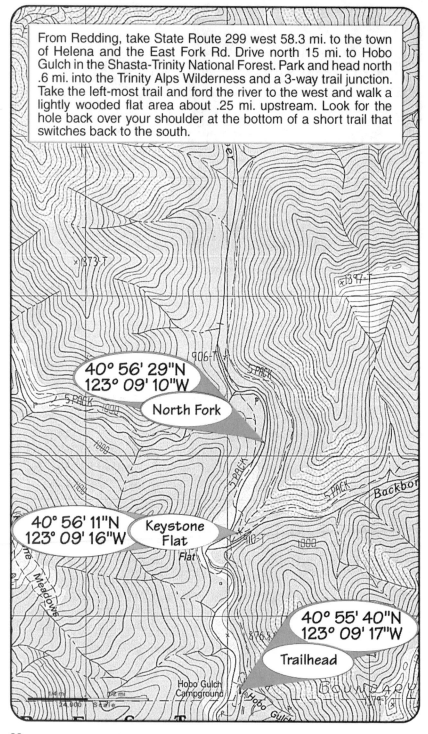

From Redding, take State Route 299 west 58.3 mi. to the town of Helena and the East Fork Rd. Drive north 15 mi. to Hobo Gulch in the Shasta-Trinity National Forest. Park and head north .6 mi. into the Trinity Alps Wilderness and a 3-way trail junction. Take the left-most trail and ford the river to the west and walk a lightly wooded flat area about .25 mi. upstream. Look for the hole back over your shoulder at the bottom of a short trail that switches back to the south.

40° 56' 29"N
123° 09' 10"W

North Fork

40° 56' 11"N
123° 09' 16"W

Keystone
Flat

40° 55' 40"N
123° 09' 17"W

Trailhead

North Fork
Trinity River

Here's one if you're on your way to the high country in the Trinity Alps. Mostly a sun and splash spot. The pool is about 50 feet long, formed by a minor bend in the river. A rock finger puts the jog in the river and behind the rock is an eddy with water six to eight feet deep. It's a nice place to sun and there are low ledges you can jump off. No big vertical, though. Lots of cars parked at the Hobo Gulch trailhead. Lots of people hiking to the high country. Lots of hoof prints and horse manure from the pack stock. Fortunately the pool isn't visible from the trail, so most people walk right by. Privacy is good. The pool is only fair on its merits, but worth mentioning since the trail is really nice. Most of it's well shaded and excellent for a trail run.

Apparently the shade wasn't as good during the days pack trains supplied high country miners along the Backbone Trail. A man known as Hobo Dick became crazed with the heat and ran the five miles from the top of the ridge to the then–unnamed gulch. Once at the North Fork of the Trinity he submersed his head and started gulping the cold water, according to a 1937 story in the Trinity Journal of Weaverville. And that's where they found him, dead. He was buried up the ridge and the area surrounding the Backbone and North Fork trails was named Hobo Gulch.

From Redding, take State Route 299 west 51.75 mi. to Canyon Creek Rd. in the Shasta-Trinity National Forest. Turn north 12.9 mi. to the trailhead in the Trinity Alps Wilderness. Hike north on trail 10W08, climbing 1,735 vertical feet in 3.7 mi. to the top of Canyon Creek Falls. From the first pool at the top of the main fall, boulder hop 10 minutes downstream to the lip. Forty feet of minor 3rd class scrambling gets you down to the first pool below the fall, which is generally too fast to swim in. Descend farther to the left to a second pool that's only fair on its merits, but it has the fall for a front yard view. Very nice.

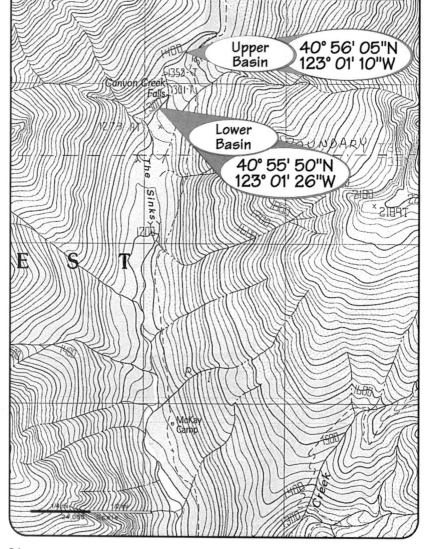

Upper Basin
40° 56' 05"N
123° 01' 10"W

Lower Basin
40° 55' 50"N
123° 01' 26"W

Canyon Creek

Extremely heavy use along this trail. With as many as 50 cars at the trailhead, you wonder how in the world you could find a semiprivate swimming hole. Everybody stops just above the main fall at a 20-foot-high cascade that bounces down granite ledges into a pool eight to ten feet deep. Privacy factor is nil up here. Down below the fall the pools aren't quite as nice, but *way* more private. Few people, laden as most are with backpacks, will venture the trip over the fall lip. Here's the secret: It's not that gnarly. Forty feet of minor third class scrambling gets you down.

The first pool of the main falls is churning and dangerous. Use extreme caution. The best pools are farther down. Ledges around the main falls are really nice, four to five feet wide and composed of right angles. However lots of mist coming off falls make them awfully cool. Water gets up to the mid 60s owing to the surrounding rock and southern exposure. Probably best later in the season. Although the main face of the fall is visible to hikers headed up the trail, the pools below it are not, so you can rely on good to excellent privacy. And what a view over your shoulder at the fall.

The scramble to the left of the falls (as you face downstream) isn't a rappel, but any members of the party without rock climbing experience might want a rope. Plenty of trees for anchors, no hardware necessary.

From Redding take State Route 299 west 58.3 mi. to the town of Helena and the East Fork Rd. (County Road 412) Drive north 1.3 mi. to the bridge over the North Fork Trinity River. Park just outside the Trinity Alps Wilderness and walk 10 minutes upstream on the right bank.

40°47' 14"N
123°08' 06"W

Paradise

Bridge

Paradise Pools

Best thing to say about this spot: It's a good place to meet people. It's not unusual to find 30 or 40 folks here where a series of pools lead down to the highway bridge. The best pool is up around a curve in the river where water comes down a 15-foot baffle of serpentine. The entire hole is 40 to 50 feet long. A finger of serpentine sticks about 30 feet out into the main channel. The deepest part is in the eddy behind the rock finger. The sides of the hole are remarkably round with easy ledges to pull yourself out of the water for repeated trips to the adjoining jumping rock. No sand beach, but plenty of ledges, lots of sun.

A second hole called Big Paradise lies upstream. It's actually the smaller of the two and more bouldery, but with a much larger jumping rock, about 75 feet. The sweet spot is tiny. Still, there are those who jump into it. The splatter potential is way high. I wouldn't do it with a gun to my head.

Water quality looks good; however, locals say gold dredgers upstream periodically turn the water muddy. Significant brown algae and moss on the river rocks. Very slippery. Must get really fuzzy later in the season when the water heats up.

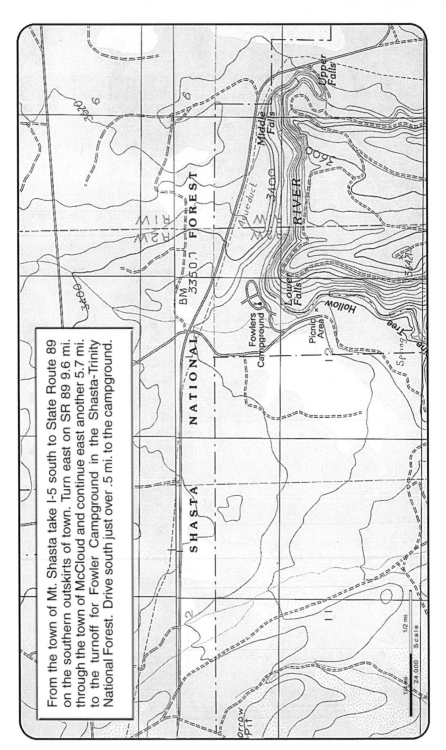

From the town of Mt. Shasta take I-5 south to State Route 89 on the southern outskirts of town. Turn east on SR 89 9.6 mi. through the town of McCloud and continue east another 5.7 mi. to the turnoff for Fowler Campground in the Shasta-Trinity National Forest. Drive south just over .5 mi. to the campground.

SHASTA NATIONAL FOREST

BM 3350.7

RIVER

Upper Falls

Middle Falls

Lower Falls

Aqueduct

3400

1600

3427

Fowlers Campground

Picnic Area

Hollow

Spring Tree

1/4 mi   1/2 mi

24,000   Scale

Borrow Pit

68

McCloud Falls

If rivers could walk, this one would swagger. Three tall, proud falls empty into deep holes, all of them surrounded by dark volcanic rock from nearby Mt. Shasta. The upper falls is gorgeous stone, 92 feet high that comes down in two steps to an enormous, round hole about 100 feet in diameter. Below, the water moves briskly through boulders and elephant ear a little less than half a mile to the middle fall which itself is 81 feet tall and 100 feet wide. It plunges in an uneven curtain into an oval pool filled with dark, Gothic-looking water. One or two nice rocks to dive from. Many swim across the pool on the right-hand side where a boulder pile leads up to the fall itself. Water is mid 60s in summer. Seating is on boulders, none of them terribly flat, none big enough to lie down on. The lower falls is a drive-up and filled with people. The expectation of privacy is only slightly better at the first two falls.

Regrettably all of the falls are too recessed to have views of Mt. Shasta and too accessible to be really wild. If only McCloud River were some remote watershed it would be worthy of highest honors. There's a bright spot to the river's easy approachability. The trail is being reconstructed to the standards of the Americans with Disabilities Act.

A word of caution: many nonexpert anglers visit here. Lots of them snag and break their line. Any line you encounter may have hooks in it.

Why Bother

Man Hole
Coffee Creek just above Clair Engle Reservoir. Drive-up, family place. Big sand and gravel beach, lots and lots of people.

Emerald Pools
Pretty little cascade coming down in five chutes, but you practically have to sit down to submerge your shoulders.

Ney Springs Creek
Lots of rock fall fills the creek.

Mossbrae Falls
Really gorgeous, but the train track runs right by it and the rumble of a three locomotive freight effectively destroys the solitude.

Chico, Paradise &
the Feather River

In Oroville from the intersection of State Route 70 and SR 162, drive SR 70 north 6.5 mi. to the intersection with SR 149. Bear right, still on SR 70 for 28 mi., past the Cresta Dam and another 2.4 mi. to Rock Creek. For lower Rock Creek park at a small turnout and follow a game trail 20 minutes upstream on the right bank. Climb briefly to a couple of laurel trees, then back to the creek and boulder hop upstream to the hole. For Middle Rock Creek, continue past that lower parking area for .5 mi. to a second turnout. An abandoned dirt road climbs gently for .25 mi. to a creek crossing below the waterslide. Follow slabs up to the main fall. For Upper Rock Creek continue upstream on the left to where the creek runs from the northeast. Another 300 yds leads to a grotto with a small deep pool. To the left are a couple of boulders that appear impassible. Up under them you will find a wiggle through passage that leads to the hole.

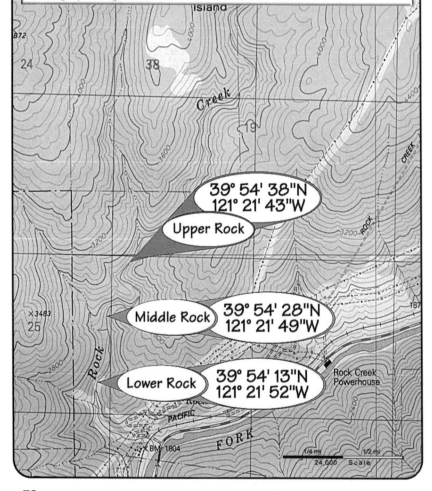

Upper Rock — 39° 54' 38"N 121° 21' 43"W

Middle Rock — 39° 54' 28"N 121° 21' 49"W

Lower Rock — 39° 54' 13"N 121° 21' 52"W

Rock Creek Powerhouse

Lower Rock Creek

After a short climb up the canyon, a trail descends to the creek where there are a variety of approach options. Climbers can traverse right around a wall. Scramblers can go left across a slab, and smart people just walk straight up the creek. It's a swimming hole; you might as well get wet.

The main feature is a 20-foot falls pouring over a slab facing directly south. Lots of boulders in the pool, but good and deep in the middle, as much as 20 feet. Good walls on both sides make the hole feel nice and cozy. The right wall is about 80 feet, the left wall is around 60 feet. Lounging is on a boulder jumble, the best of which is a fifty-square-foot monster directly downstream from the foot of the fall. Slabs to the left offer more space, but they are tilted at a steepish angle.

Lots of granite domes around the Feather River. Cycles of heating and cooling combined with rain are at least in part responsible for the exfoliation that produces the domes. When water is added to feldspar it forms clay which swells when wet then crumbles when dry. And since feldspar crystals are longer in one direction, that helps orient the cracks.

Bonus feature: The wall on the right side below the hole has rappel slings at the top and it's bolted with some very old hangars. Kinda sketchy since the hangars appear to be homemade.

Rock Creek

Middle Rock Creek

A waterpark of Olympian beauty. Broad shade hangs over huge, unjointed granite slabs which contain four holes, each having its own season and character. The lowest hole is the catch for an 80-foot waterslide. Above the slide is a magnificent diving hole. Then a short scramble above the diving hole are some exquisite clothing optional tubs and farther still is the upper fall where late in the year you can get under the cascade and be pounded by water.

Late spring through early summer is peak season for the slide says William Cooper, a Rock Creek regular. More water keeps your butt from bouncing on the rockbed. The diving pool is best in the summer when there's lots of shade and the water is up in the mid 60s – perfect conditions to practice the slack grace of the "Cooper gainer," a loosely tucked back flip the Arkansas native has worked his life to perfect. "I just started when I was a kid, doing back flips on my bed at home. I went on to where I could do it off the roof of the house into the swimming pool. Now I can do it from just about anything, I guess." A note on the water slide. It's tough to exit the churning pool with an innertube. To get out, chuck the tube upstream into an eddy, then clamber onto the narrow ledge to your right. When the tube comes around grab it. Don't worry, it shouldn't wash over.

Little North Fork

Upper
Rock Creek

Listen up lipophobes. Here's a swimming hole that discriminates against fat people. To reach it you have to scramble between a couple of closely spaced, cabin-sized boulders. On the other side you'll find two high rock walls, both of them 75 feet tall with a narrow chute of water between them. Looking left up the wall you'll see a crack that's uncleaned, mossy and leads to a narrow ledge where an oak tree guards a 50-foot view straight down the well shaft into the hole. The water is around 15 feet deep in the middle. The hem of the pool is formed by a couple of slabs and some boulders that have fallen into the water opposite the fall. There's no beach adjoining it, but there is a pretty sand pocket just on the other side of the fat filter.

Even over the roar of the water you'll hear the call of the American dipper, a slate gray songbird that makes its home on fast streams throughout California. Dippers are a diving bird, but without the characteristic webbed feet. They feed on aquatic insects by diving to the bottom of streams and running along the gravel with its wings half open in a unique feeding behavior. Also of interest, the dippers build their nests behind waterfalls for protection. If ever there was a swimming hole mascot, this is it.

You may want to pause on the way up at a grotto with all sorts of little potholes and a rock bridge forming the impound of a small, deep pool. A kind spot to get in the water and bob.

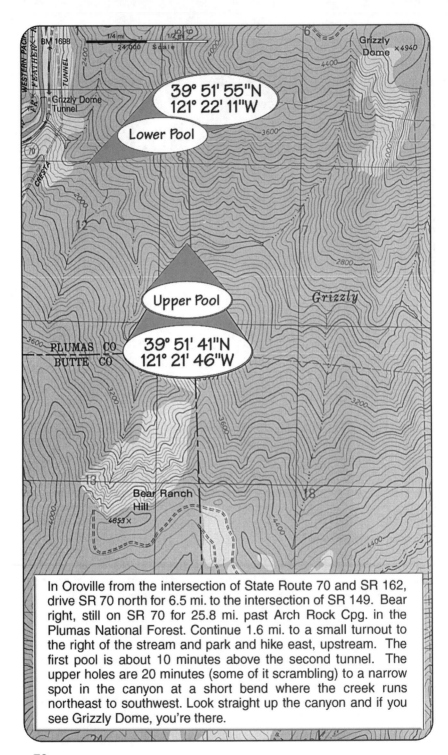

39° 51' 55"N
121° 22' 11"W

Lower Pool

Upper Pool

39° 51' 41"N
121° 21' 46"W

PLUMAS CO
BUTTE CO

Grizzly Dome ×4940

Grizzly

Bear Ranch Hill

In Oroville from the intersection of State Route 70 and SR 162, drive SR 70 north for 6.5 mi. to the intersection of SR 149. Bear right, still on SR 70 for 25.8 mi. past Arch Rock Cpg. in the Plumas National Forest. Continue 1.6 mi. to a small turnout to the right of the stream and park and hike east, upstream. The first pool is about 10 minutes above the second tunnel. The upper holes are 20 minutes (some of it scrambling) to a narrow spot in the canyon at a short bend where the creek runs northeast to southwest. Look straight up the canyon and if you see Grizzly Dome, you're there.

Grizzly Creek

A series of pools form where the creek works its way northeast. The first is a nice round pond at the bottom of a short rapid. Amusements here include hanging onto a submerged rock lip at the bottom of the rapids and holding yourself under the swift water until your ears beat against your head. Nice slabs to sit on, but little shade. It's about a ten-minute walk. More with a cooler.

The main pool is a 20-minute scramble farther upstream. Minor third class scrambling with ledges and pockets delivers you to a narrow piece of water about 150 feet long. The sides are bounded by moss-covered diving rocks. A rope leads up the left face. Getting up to the diving rocks is something of a blister and the trip down can be even worse. The sweet spot is awfully narrow because submerged ledges stick out well into the main channel of water.

Grizzly Creek is perhaps the most unusual approach option in this book. Instead of wading the 200 or so yards from the highway to the first pool, try the tunnels just to the right of the small parking area. The first tunnel is 70 feet long and although the opening is large enough to walk through, the ceiling lowers to four feet. Definitely some crouching going on. The second tunnel is more challenging. It bends, so there's no light for about half of its 80 foot length. Water in the tunnels should be about knee-deep.

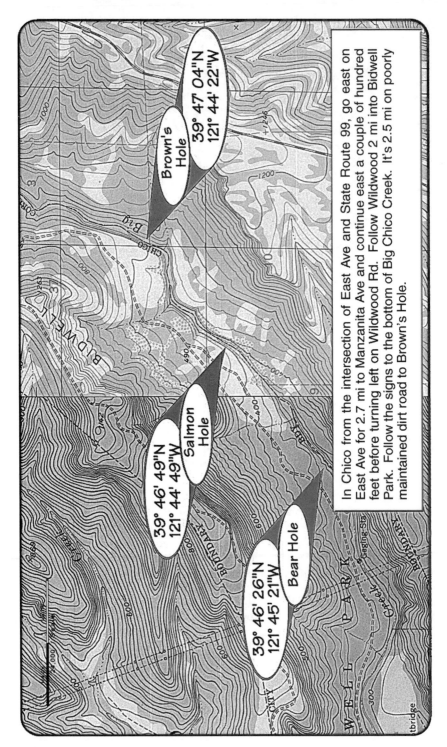

In Chico from the intersection of East Ave and State Route 99, go east on East Ave for 2.7 mi to Manzanita Ave and continue east a couple of hundred feet before turning left on Wildwood Rd. Follow Wildwood 2 mi into Bidwell Park. Follow the signs to the bottom of Big Chico Creek. It's 2.5 mi on poorly maintained dirt road to Brown's Hole.

Brown's Hole
39° 47' 04"N
121° 44' 22"W

Salmon Hole
39° 46' 49"N
121° 44' 49"'W

Bear Hole
39° 46' 26"N
121° 45' 21"W

Brown's Hole

Upper and lower holes. The upper is fed by a six-foot stairstep fall. The pool is a strapping 100 feet long, but only 20 feet wide with irregular sides and bottom. Nice large pool, shame the bottom isn't less boulder-choked. The lower pool is about 80 yards long and punctuated by a rope swing which deposits riders into water 10 feet deep.

You'll find four sand beaches around the lower pool on the downstream side. Best way to get to them is swim. Brown's Hole, by virtue of its remote upstream location, is the only place on Big Chico Creek that on weekends doesn't swarm with college students from Chico State. Attendance averages ten or so people on a weekend, but that can go as high as 40!

The rock on Big Chico is very interesting. It's a lava flow 18 million years old and full of pockets both big and small. Down at Bear Hole there are tunnels you can swim through.

In Paradise from the intersection of Skyway and State Route 191, drive north on Skyway 12.6 mi. to Sterling City and Reston Rd. Follow Reston (aka P&R line, aka Forest Service 24N04) east, then south to a fork. Stay right at the fork onto Robley Point Rd. (aka P-line, aka FS 24N03). Drive 5 mi. to the bridge over Big Kimshew Creek in the Plumas National Forest. The falls are northeast of the bridge. For Yellow Dog, continue less than .5 mi. up P-line to a roadside turnout on the right. A steep rocky road, owned by a lumber company, descends to the river. Walk downstream on the left bank a little less than 1.25 mi. to the falls.

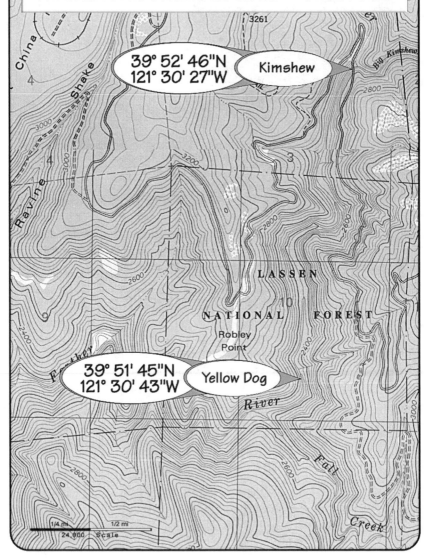

39° 52' 46"N
121° 30' 27"W — Kimshew

39° 51' 45"N
121° 30' 43"W — Yellow Dog

LASSEN

NATIONAL   FOREST

Robley
Point

Kimshew Falls

A big, open hole with a tall wide fall. Locals say the water is 30 feet deep under the fall. I didn't have time to jump in and confirm the claim, but I'm skeptical. Nevertheless, diving is fabulous. On the left hand side jumps are 10, 15 and 20 feet. The rock is even taller on the right with jumps at 25 and 40 feet. Better still, it's easy to clamber back to the top after each jump. Water quality was good with visibility about six feet or so. Lots of boulders to sit on. No real place to lie down, though.

Since Kimshew is less than 100 yards from the road the crowd is more representative of the general public than you'll find at swimming holes where you have to hike in. More pickup trucks and NRA stickers. If you want to fit in, remove the public radio license plate frame from your car, bring an air mattress and lite beer. Still, since it's basically a drive-up, this is a good destination for families with pre-schoolers.

Many of the roads in the area are light rail right of ways that were built to haul out the virgin timber. Although falls are on forest service land, much of the surrounding property is still owned by logging companies. Much of it has been harvested recently.

Mountain Dog

Yellow Dog

If the sound of big water scares you, don't come here. It roars into a gorge that churns and throbs like the inside of a washing machine. Vertical walls are 200 feet tall on the far side and a mere 45 feet on the near side. The shorter wall is the one that's galvanizing, because you have to descend it on a homemade rope ladder and then traverse to get into the sheer-sided hole. The hole itself is about 70 feet long and 30 feet wide. Numerous diving platforms, but with submerged ledges. Water's in the mid 60s. A pale, water-polished finger of rock projects into the lower part of the hole creating a perfect lounging spot. It's about the only place to sit and getting there is somewhat involved.

Finding the trailhead in the maze of unmarked roads crisscrossing the privately owned timberland is daunting. When you do reach the fall, the trail (such as it is) appears to end. To continue, go up over a steep, short granite slab to the left and you'll find the rope ladder. When you get to the bottom of the ladder the traverse leads to the right where you need to reach out to a rope that's a little scary. It's fixed in a crack by means of a railroad spike and some putty! But, what the hell. At that point the drop is only seven feet and you land in the water anyway.

Some old graffiti reduces the overall rating from classic to excellent. Moderate to heavy bushwhacking. If you're fussy you might want to wear boots.

From Oroville, take State Route 162 north 26 mi. to the Brush Creek Ranger Station in the Plumas National Forest. Continue north on Forest Service 119 to FS 60. Continue north 9 mi. over pretty crappy road. Look for the descending trail about 200 yds before the wooden bridge that leads to Little North Fork Cpg.

Little North Fork

So deep it's menacing. A couple of adjoining rock faces lean out over an L-shaped abyss creating 25 and 35-foot jumps into a mondo tank of water. I don't think you'd hit bottom if you dropped an I-beam end first. A tall, narrow impound at the bottom of the L is responsible for the depth. It's one of the clearest, sharpest, steepest impounds I've seen and a damn nice piece of rock to stretch out on and catch noonday sun after a chilly dip in the deep end. Notice on the opposite bank a projection of highly folded metamorphic rock in which the softer material has eroded away leaving a sort of herring-bone pattern. Fair expectation of privacy, but it's close to the road so you will find some cigarette butts and lite beer cans.

Better chance of being alone at a pool 250 yards downstream. I only saw one pair of footprints in the sand pockets there. It's only 15 to 20 feet in diameter with some boulders on the bottom. The pool itself is created by a low, west-facing ridge that forces a bend in the water. Excellent water. Although the road is a mere 50 yards up a steep hill, it's not visible from the hole because of heavy vegetation. Nice for a couple of people to get in and splash about. I'd call it good. Also check out an elephant ear fringed pool visible downstream. The foot approach is very short, although steep and on loose dirt. The real annoyance is the drive, almost ten miles on really lousy dirt road. Leave your Corvette at home.

Why Bother

Butte Creek
Great rock, but too many gold dredges make the water murky.

Frey Creek
Feather Falls National Recreation Trail. Small pools.

Buzzard's Roost
High school party spot. Amazing vertical, but disgusting with litter.

Bear Hole
Extremely interesting basalt, but I've seen fewer people at a Dodges game.

Salmon Hole
Ditto. Really cool, but filled with students fromCall State Chico.

Motherlode & Northern Sierra

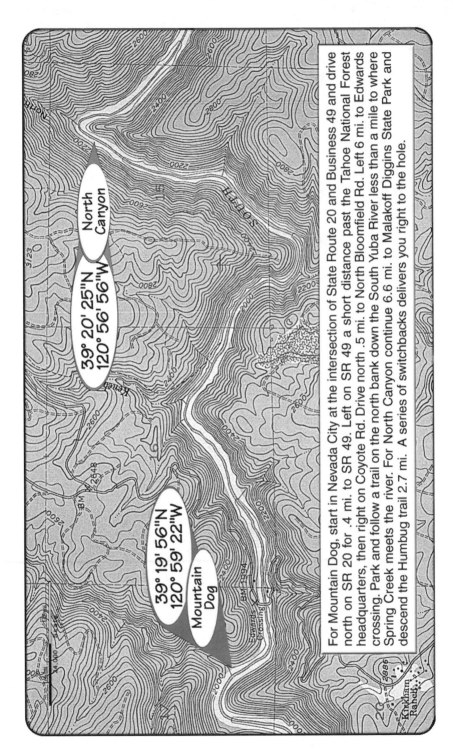

For Mountain Dog, start in Nevada City at the intersection of State Route 20 and Business 49 and drive north on SR 20 for .4 mi. to SR 49. Left on SR 49 a short distance past the Tahoe National Forest headquarters, then right on Coyote Rd. Drive north .5 mi. to North Bloomfield Rd. Left 6 mi. to Edwards crossing. Park and follow a trail on the north bank down the South Yuba River less than a mile to where Spring Creek meets the river. For North Canyon continue 6.6 mi. to Malakoff Diggins State Park and descend the Humbug trail 2.7 mi. A series of switchbacks delivers you right to the hole.

North Canyon
39° 20' 25"N
120° 56' 56"W

Mountain Dog
39° 19' 56"N
120° 59' 22"W

Photo: Paul Harton

Mammoth Hole

A big, fat patch of water. Measuring more than 100 yards in diameter, Mammoth is wide enough to swim laps. There's a low wall you use as a diving platform, but you're better off to treat this hole like a nice, friendly lake. It's open and sunny, a great place to spend the hot part of the day bobbing up and down with your beverage of choice. Unfortunately, there's little area for lounging. There *is* a small bench and sand bar on the opposite shore, but you have to swim to get there. Consider bringing an air mattress or innertube even though both are a little bourgeois.

Yours may not be the only flotation device on the river. Small, floating dredges are a popular way to look for gold and several claim operators have formed semi permanent camp up the road at Shenanigan Flat. Since claim operators believe any piece of junk could prove useful in the future, pipe, barrels, tents and tarpaulins create a blight. Nevertheless it can be instructive to stroll through the camp and compare contemporary miners to the '49er archetype of a sourdough with a pan and shovel.

Despite the miners, the expectation of privacy is good. Mammoth has a long season since the width of the hole creates a slow current during early high water and the western exposure creates warm, sunny autumn afternoons. Water quality is a little hinky.

West Clear Creek

part of *Southwestern
Swimming Holes*, a survey
of 200 creeks and canyons
from the high plateaus of
Utah to the Mexican border.

Cherokee Creek

The place to be when the mercury tops 100. The 12-foot fall that churns into the tub below creates spindrift that, as it evaporates, cools the air by as much as 10 degrees. As you drop into the stream you'll notice the temperature changes immediately. The steep canyon walls give Cherokee Creek Fall a great feeling of being in your own little room. Tall trees add to the sense of being inside while outdoors.

One tree in particular stands out. It's an enormous, old growth white fir about half way along the trail from the footbridge to the fall. The thing is huge given that most of the area's been logged repeatedly since mining days. Also look for rock walls, evidence of the shacks miners built before the advent of travel trailers that are so broadly represented in the mining camp at Shenanigan Flats.

Although people apparently know about this place, it doesn't seem too heavily visited. You may encounter the stray cigarette butt, piece of litter or wads of tissue. One of the miners up the road at Shenanigan Flats said he's cleaned the place up several times after inconsiderate users built campfires. Nevertheless, he said he had visited the hole almost one dozen times and never encountered anyone else there, so the expectation of privacy is excellent. The drainage points due south, so it stays warm later in the season than you might expect.

From the corner of State Route 20 and Business 49 in Nevada City, drive north on SR 20 for .4 mi. to SR 49. Left for 14 mi. to the bridge over the Middle Yuba River. Cross and take an immediate left on Moonshine Creek Rd. Drive 1 mi. and park, being sure not to block any driveways. There's lots of private property, so obey signs. Look for a trail on the left. The river is .5 mi. downhill where you'll find an overused hole named Strawberry. Mushroom is 250 yds. farther downstream. For Oregon Creek go 1 mi. north of the Middle Yuba bridge. Park on the east side of SR 49 at a two-car turnout, walk five minutes downhill and you're there.

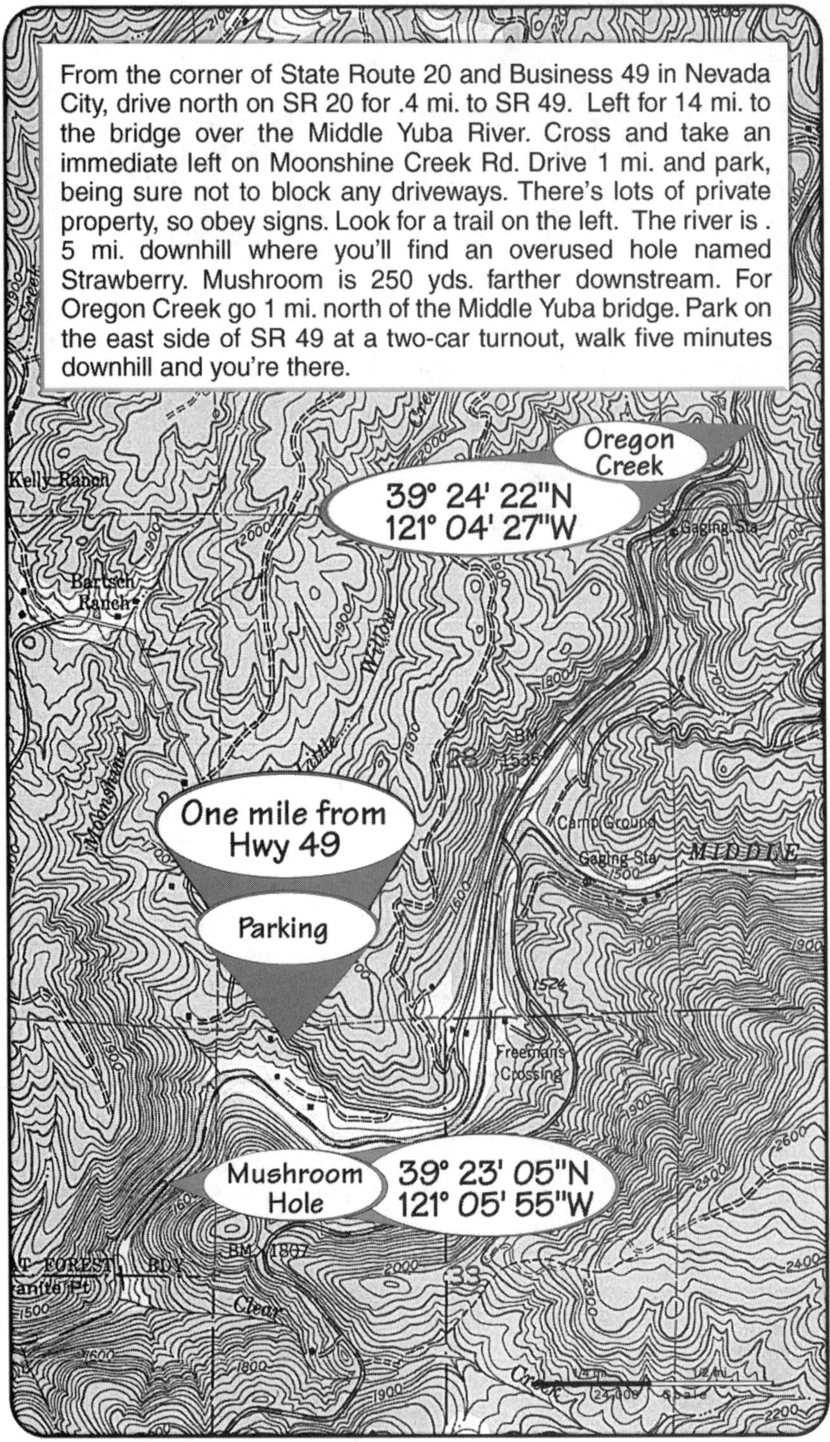

Oregon Creek

39° 24' 22"N
121° 04' 27"W

One mile from Hwy 49

Parking

Mushroom Hole

39° 23' 05"N
121° 05' 55"W

Oregon Creek

A Sierra classic. Oregon Creek is awfully darn close to being the perfect swimming hole. It's hidden, yet accessible. It's deep, but not too narrow. It mixes square blocks of granite with the sinuous curves of water-worn rock. These combinations make Oregon Creek a delight. The upper tub is fed by a pair of small falls. One descends in perfect stair steps; the other is composed of three spouts that braid together as they tumble into the pool. Farther below, right-angle rock fissures produce swimming holes, some of them perpendicular as poured concrete. Conversely, the rock up above is etched in smooth, sculptural lines with so many different grooves that watching the water flow over it is mesmerizing. There's not much of a sandbar to sit on, but the surrounding rock is evenly cut in four-foot-wide terraces that make the area look like an amphitheater. It has some awesome Sierra Jacuzzis and a waterfall you can duck behind and stare out through a cool curtain of running water.

Located as it is on a local watershed, Oregon Creek isn't prone to becoming a raging torrent since it doesn't drain snow runoff from the High Sierra. You can basically use this hole as soon as the water's warm enough. There's plenty of shade although probably not a lot of privacy. The approach is gentle, but the slabs that lead down to the water are steep and polished. Submerged rocks have caused several neck injuries in years past. Learn where they are before you jump.

Mushroom Hole

Photo: Paul Harton

Mushroom Hole

Ask locals where the good swimming holes are and this place always comes up. The hole takes its name from a 45-foot, mushroom shaped rock that's a favorite jumping off spot for the cliff diving set. The vertical is really great and the landing is plenty deep. It's a wet approach and that keeps some of the people away, but not many. You'll find at least one dozen individuals here on a weekend and not a heck of a lot of room for them to sit either.

On the way to Mushroom, at the bottom of the spur trail, is a popular swimming hole called Strawberry. It's over-visited, suffering litter, graffiti and dozens of people. Can be a rowdy crowd and some inevitably make it down to Mushroom where the true locals are more sedate. Pools that look so enticing to us are also attractive to pond turtles, a sensitive species. Turtles reproduce slowly and let's face it, if you looked like a turtle you'd be lucky to get any either. When you visit take care to walk on bare rocks, where possible. Turtles lay eggs in the sand as well as decaying vegetation. If it looks like turtles could dig in it, try not to disturb it.

The frogs and turtles tolerate the summer time yahoos and the occasional beer can that floats downstream from Strawberry. Land owners on the adjoining property are less liberal, so obey the no trespassing signs.

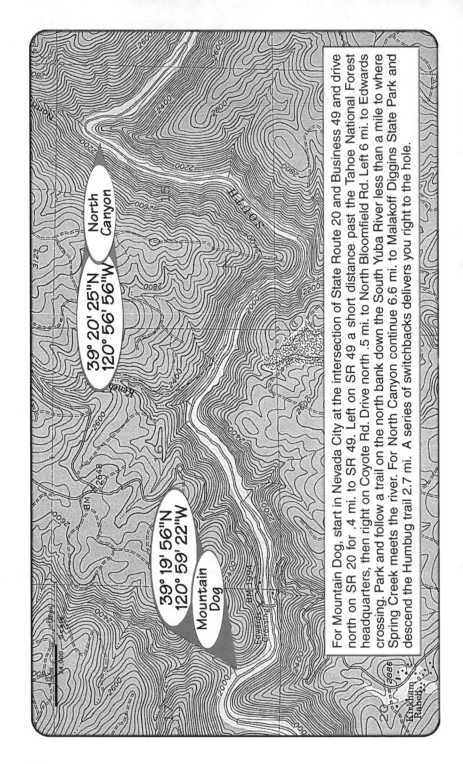

North Canyon

39° 20' 25"N
120° 56' 56"W

39° 19' 56"N
120° 59' 22"W

Mountain Dog

For Mountain Dog, start in Nevada City at the intersection of State Route 20 and Business 49 and drive north on SR 20 for .4 mi. to SR 49. Left on SR 49 a short distance past the Tahoe National Forest headquarters, then right on Coyote Rd. Drive north .5 mi. to North Bloomfield Rd. Left 6 mi. to Edwards crossing. Park and follow a trail on the north bank down the South Yuba River less than a mile to where Spring Creek meets the river. For North Canyon continue 6.6 mi. to Malakoff Diggins State Park and descend the Humbug trail 2.7 mi. A series of switchbacks delivers you right to the hole.

Photo: Paul Harton

North Canyon

North Canyon is really a series of holes within a long constriction. From the trail the hole stands out like a jewel in the rocky canyon below. It's located at a bend in the river, but this one's a big, 150-degree turn. There's a broad, rocky ledge above the river with plenty of room to spread out. Diving is pretty good, not more than 15 vertical feet, but the diving rocks are easily climbed for repeated plunges.

These days the water runs clear. That was not always the case. The Yuba was a mess in 1884 as placer miners diverted water to work dry areas like the Malakoff Diggins just above North Canyon. To separate the gold they sluiced vast amounts of gravel through chutes. The tailings were flushed downstream into the Yuba, eventually coming to rest on top of valuable agricultural land in the valley below. Farmers sued the mining companies, winning a decision that ultimately ended hydraulic mining altogether and codified what's now considered America's first environmental law.

Like most places on the Yuba, early season water levels will be dangerously high, especially if it's been a heavy snow year. It's going to be cold also. Best wait until July or so. The expectation of privacy is fair. The broad terrace attracts visitors and the Malakoff Diggins State Park brings many people down the South Yuba Trail toward North Canyon.

Mountain Dog

Photo: Paul Harton

Mountain Dog

The river under the Edward's Crossing bridge gets pretty crowded. More discriminating bathers spread out to one of the holes along the South Yuba Trail between the Edward's and Purdon Crossing. Mountain Dog is one that gets a little less activity. It's a sweet place with a kiddie pool. An unnamed creek creates the twin spout emptying 15 feet into a shallow gravel basin. The adult pool is slightly downstream. It's about 60 feet in diameter with a comfortable gravel bar. The water is ten feet deep at best, but bring a snorkel for entertainment, 'cause there's nothing to jump from.

This is a swimming hole for the practical minded — very pleasant, user friendly and easy to find — but not something that's going to take your breath away. This is more of a family swimming place since access is easy. However, as with any of the hike-in spots on the South Yuba, it's not uncommon to find skinny dippers. If you bring junior, be prepared to give an anatomy lesson.

On the trail right below Edward's Crossing you'll find a cheery, hand painted sign that reads "Right to pass by permission." An easy-going landowner willing to let the public cross private property must post a sign to let people know that they are crossing private land. Otherwise the owner could lose rights to that land.

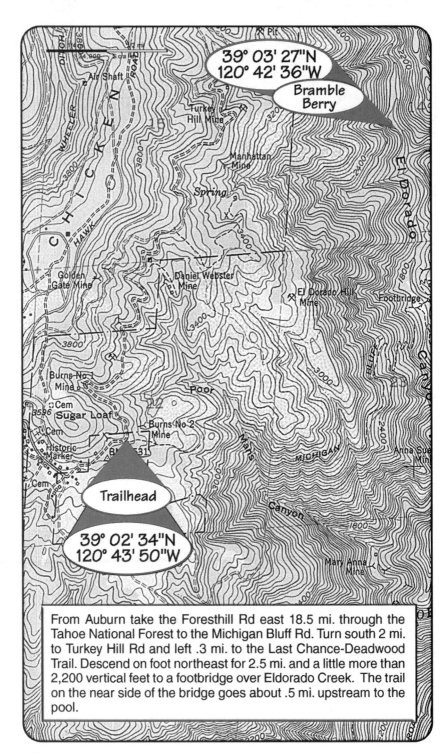

39° 03' 27"N
120° 42' 36"W

Bramble Berry

Trailhead

39° 02' 34"N
120° 43' 50"W

From Auburn take the Foresthill Rd east 18.5 mi. through the Tahoe National Forest to the Michigan Bluff Rd. Turn south 2 mi. to Turkey Hill Rd and left .3 mi. to the Last Chance-Deadwood Trail. Descend on foot northeast for 2.5 mi. and a little more than 2,200 vertical feet to a footbridge over Eldorado Creek. The trail on the near side of the bridge goes about .5 mi. upstream to the pool.

Bramble Berry

Dark slate streaked with quartz gives this hole an engaging striped look. The lower pool is a 60-foot rectangle formed by steep, even slabs of dark Calaveras formation. A broad, white seam of quartz runs straight down the bottom of the pool as if someone painted it on. The upper pool has a few nice rock terraces along the east side for relaxing, but don't expect to improve your tan here. Located as it is at the bottom of a canyon, the shade is deep enough for bracken ferns which add considerably to the swimming hole's character.

The trail to Bramble Berry is part of the famed Western States Endurance Run, a 100-mile death march across the Sierra from Squaw Valley to Auburn. This is one of deepest canyons the runners cross. It's a 2,100 foot vertical climb to the top of the trail then another 40 or so miles to the finish of the race. Consider that temperatures are sometimes around 100 degrees on race day and you can imagine how tempting it is to jump in the water and stay there.

The expectation of privacy is good since most potential bathers are diverted by the pool directly under the footbridge. A warm day in late autumn is a great time to visit and graze for blackberries on the eastern bank of the creek. I visited on Thanksgiving and gorged until my fingers were stained purple and the dark juice ran down my wrists.

From Auburn take the Foresthill Rd east 41.7 mi. through the Tahoe National Forest to Sailor Flat Rd. Turn north 1.6 mi. to the Sailor Flat trailhead. Descend trail 13E30 2.5 mi. and 2,230 vertical feet to the North Fork of the American River. Vertigo is 1.5 mi. downstream. Or if you prefer, you can stop at some good pools immediately downstream from the spur trail.

Vertigo
39° 13' 19"N
120° 31' 24"W

Canyon Bottom
39° 13' 01"N
120° 29' 50"W

Vertigo

Do you dare? The cliffs here are 50 feet high and more—sheer rock rising out of coke-bottle green water that may or may not be deep enough to arrest a body falling at more than 40 m.p.h. I wouldn't know because I was way too chicken to try. Fortunately there's plenty more to occupy your attention at this excellent swimming hole. More than 100 yards long, it's deep and the surrounding cliffs make it seem like a high-ceilinged corridor of some European palace. There's a nice bench of land on the southern bank, perfect for picnicking. The best recommendation is to get there early and bring a fishing rod. Spend the morning drowning a few worms and the afternoon soaking yourself.

There are submerged rocks, so if you dive, aim for the sweet spot because it you splatter, help is a long, long way off. Late season is the time to visit because the constriction that forms the swimming hole means that water flow is guaranteed to be dangerous except in lowest water conditions.

On the way down, you walk past an abandoned stamp mill. Motherlode rivers are amazing in this way. You'll hike a narrow trail so steep you'd swear that even with modern logistics the heaviest equipment miners could deliver to the bottom of the canyon would be a wheel barrow. Then you discover some rusted five-ton industrial arthropod that was dragged down there by men using nothing more powerful than a mule.

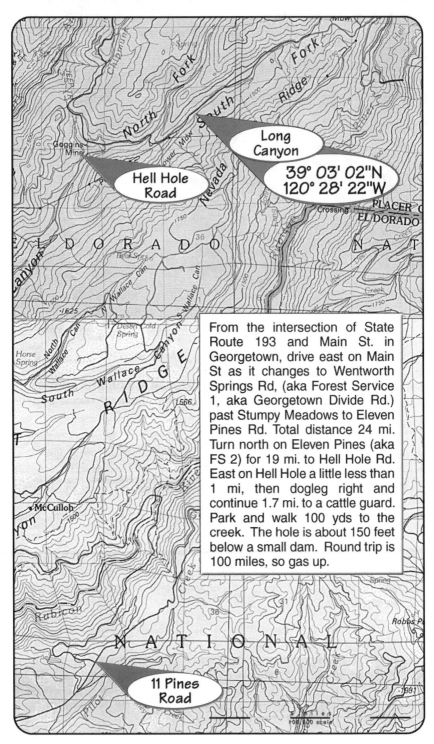

Long Canyon

**39° 03' 02"N
120° 28' 22"W**

Hell Hole Road

11 Pines Road

From the intersection of State Route 193 and Main St. in Georgetown, drive east on Main St as it changes to Wentworth Springs Rd, (aka Forest Service 1, aka Georgetown Divide Rd.) past Stumpy Meadows to Eleven Pines Rd. Total distance 24 mi. Turn north on Eleven Pines (aka FS 2) for 19 mi. to Hell Hole Rd. East on Hell Hole a little less than 1 mi, then dogleg right and continue 1.7 mi. to a cattle guard. Park and walk 100 yds to the creek. The hole is about 150 feet below a small dam. Round trip is 100 miles, so gas up.

Long Canyon

If there was an award for the swimming hole with the best lines, this would probably be it. A perfect kidney shape makes Long Canyon look like it could be sunk in someone's back yard with a barbecue kettle parked pool side. Long Canyon is a narrow granite channel in which the rock is on the same plane as the water flow and that's part of what makes the lines so even and unbroken. A 10-foot fall creates the pool which is about 45 feet on its major axis. Only problem is the deep end and the shallow end are reversed. It's kind of shallow next to the falls where the best jumping spot would be and at the opposite end, where there is no vertical to mention, the water is eight to ten feet deep. Strong afternoon sun falls on ample granite slabs. Good shade on the bank above.

Even though it's right next to the road and just below a campground, Long Canyon is largely undisturbed. And this place has seen *lots* of human habitation. Archeological evidence dates back 4,000 years making it one of the earlier sites in the Sierra foothills. The nearby Big Meadows Campground was excavated in the 80s and archeologists date that site to 4,500 years ago. You'll still discover bedrock mortars and possibly some arrow points.

No trash even in the fire pit. Range cattle nearby may diminish water quality and the occasional beer can may float downstream from a little-used campground.

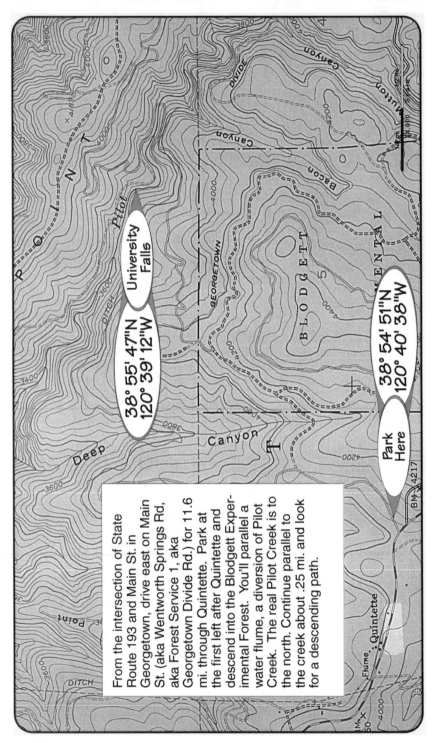

From the intersection of State Route 193 and Main St. in Georgetown, drive east on Main St. (aka Wentworth Springs Rd, aka Forest Service 1, aka Georgetown Divide Rd.) for 11.6 mi. through Quintette. Park at the first left after Quintette and descend into the Blodgett Experimental Forest. You'll parallel a water flume, a diversion of Pilot Creek. The real Pilot Creek is to the north. Continue parallel to the creek about .25 mi. and look for a descending path.

University Falls

Another waterpark. Here the granite slabs are laid down on a parallel plane with the creek, creating long waterslides upstream and a series of curtain falls and classic swimming holes downstream. The three emerald beauties at the lower falls are deep and unmuddled by boulder clutter. They are perfectly uniform in size and shape, as if struck from the same anvil. All are lens-shaped, about 80 feet by 30 feet long and deep, 12 to 15 feet. The fall above each pool rolls over the smooth granite lip in a wide, gentle shimmer. Farther down is a fourth pool. It's in trying to get to this last pool that most injuries occur. Treat it with caution. On the other hand, you can treat the upper slides as a sort of children's area where three shallow pools connect to one another through gentle slides that have an average drop of around 12 vertical feet.

The best thing to happen to this hole was a huge gate installed at the highway which added two miles to the approach. Until then University Falls got way too much traffic and was trashed. Each year there were several injuries, almost all alcohol related. Rescuers say that number has dropped in the two years since the gate was installed. Evidently two and half miles is beyond cooler range for most yahoos. Fun mountain bike rides both ways, but it's hike-a-bike on the steep foot trail down to the river.

Why Bother

Codfish Falls

More of a visual pleasure than an irresistible swimming hole. The tub at the bottom is shallow, the sides are uneven and the stream originates in the lightly developed foothills between Interstate 80 and the river canyon. This means that unless upstream residents are unusually cautious about what they let into the runoff, water quality will not be as good as in more remote streams.

Yankee Jim's Bridge Trail

Four house sized boulders slow the American River to create the main pool. On the west bank there's a low wall that's high enough to do a somersault dive, but other than that, this place doesn't have much of a vertical description. The sides are irregular and jagged with not much space for a beach towel.

Traverse Creek

The place in the Motherlode most in need of a cleanup. An excellent hole on its merits, but it's gross with litter.

Candy Rock

Bales of litter. An excellent swimming hole also badly in need of a cleanup.

Yosemite & the Central Sierra

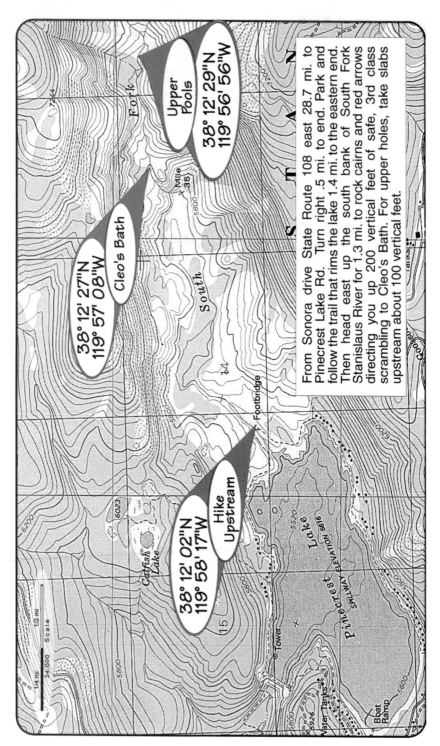

Upper Pools
38° 12' 29"N
119° 56' 56"W

Cleo's Bath
38° 12' 27"N
119° 57' 08"W

Hike Upstream
38° 12' 02"N
119° 58' 17"W

From Sonora drive State Route 108 east 28.7 mi. to Pinecrest Lake Rd. Turn right .5 mi. to end. Park and follow the trail that rims the lake 1.4 mi. to the eastern end. Then head east up the south bank of South Fork Stanislaus River for 1.3 mi. to rock cairns and red arrows directing you up 200 vertical feet of safe, 3rd class scrambling to Cleo's Bath. For upper holes, take slabs upstream about 100 vertical feet.

South Fork

Footbridge

Catfish Lake

Pinecrest Lake
SPILLWAY ELEVATION 5616

Boat Ramp

Tower

Water Tanks

Scale
1/4 mi   1/2 mi
24,000

Cleo's Bath

Steep-sided pools cored into the granite. Fun, but not too user friendly. Vertical walls in the lower two pools complicate the exit once you're in and the granite slabs are at a fairly high angle, making it uncomfortably steep and slippery for less sure-footed people. There's very limited shade and often at least one other group of people. Better to try your luck upstream where a couple of good pools don't receive as much traffic. One in particular has a fine, vertical rock impound which, as it rises out of the water to the right, creates a dandy privacy curtain where you duck to pull on your clothes if you hear people approaching upstream. Hikers coming downstream from the high country, however, will get the full show.

Several parts of this canyon were once submerged. Beginning in 1853 the forerunner of PG&E used log dams to flood three meadows as a source of water for hydraulic miners. Lake Eleanor was at 5,800 feet and Lake Gertrude was about three miles farther up the canyon. In 1916 PG&E dismantled the upper dams and replaced the lowest dam with a modern structure creating, Pinecrest Lake.

Water quality was dark and little sluggish toward the end of August. Visibility was three to four feet, which is to say, poor. It's probably better earlier in the year before warmer temperatures allow the moss to take over.

From Sonora take State Route 108 2.4 mi. east to Tuolumne Rd. and turn right. Drive 9.5 mi. to the town of Tuolumne. Take the Buchanan Rd (Forest Service 1N04) out of town 2.25 mi. to a sharp right, still on FS 1N01 for 19.2 mi., winding through the Eldorado National Forest, to the Clavey River. Park and descend on the west side of the bridge, then boulder hop 150 yds upstream to the main hole.

God's Bath

A vast, low angle slab occupies about 300 sq. ft. above a steep, narrow hole. The water is around 10 feet deep and that will remain consistent even later in the season because the impound is a vertical rock rim that's a good eight feet tall. Water enters through a narrow chute and fills a hole that is an irregular figure eight with the wide part being about 25 feet in diameter. The overwhelming element is the western wall. It rises 150 feet and makes afternoons very shady indeed. Only a sliver of sky is visible overhead.

The Clavey River is in a sort of limbo. For years environmental groups have lobbied for it to be designated a wild and scenic river. At the same time local water districts were fighting for a permit to build a dam upstream from God's Bath. That permit was eventually denied and the Forest Service agreed that it would recommend to Congress that the Clavey get special designation. That's yet another hurdle, but in the meantime the forest service is managing the river as if it were protected. That means no dams for now.

Privacy is unlikely. The approach is short, but has plenty of boulder hopping. Kids seem to dig it.

Diana
Falls

Almost a room. One-hundred eighty degrees of vertical or near vertical rock climbs 40 feet around an excellent hole. The falls are about 25 feet high with a dynamite rock impound that creates a deep, even hole in the river. Plenty of area to sit which is good because it probably sees a devil of a lot of people judging by the compaction of the trail leading to it. On the way up from the South Fork Merced you pass a couple of smaller pools and tubs that make a nice kid's area.

The name apparently derives from Roman myth. Diana, goddess of the hunt, was bathing in a pool when a hunter discovered her in all her naked loveliness. Ever the modest goddess, she turned the hunter into a stag and watched impassively as his own hounds tore him to pieces. The area around the North Fork Merced underwent a destruction of its own in 1987 when a forest fire destroyed 100,000 acres. That and the ensuing salvage logging has left the surrounding hills as nude as the goddess herself, though not nearly as pretty. Forest Service officials say the soil has remained fairly stable with only a few slips and slumps making it into the river.

Expectation of privacy is poor, however litter was not a problem when I visited.

Tuolumne River

A broad sandy bench covered with mature Ponderosa dominates the right-hand side of a hole that's six feet deep, a little more in places. It's 150 feet long and about 30 feet wide at the deep end. The structures that make it so enjoyable are several cabin sized boulders that have fallen into the stream. One, tilted at a 30-degree angle, is a big, happy rock, perfectly positioned to haul out on and soak in the sunshine. Seating on the near side is on boulders and cobbles. On the far side of the river you'll find it much more comfortable and much more private. Great to spend an entire day if not a lifetime.

A short series of switchbacks leads around the left of the first fall to a glorious fall upstream. A fire ring suggests that this hole is far from a secret, but a weekday visit should guarantee privacy. Lots of exploring and perhaps some unexpected discoveries. Chris Howard, caretaker at the Evergreen Lodge near Camp Mather recounts one surprise.

"We were fly fishing at a fish camp that fisherman have been using for 100 years or more. Something deep in a rock crevice caught my eye. I reached down in there and found a couple of old, half-empty bottles, one mescal and one brandy."

The liquor was vastly improved by the decades spent there, he said. However, the day's fishing was pretty much shot.

Candy Rock

More Tuolumne

A swimming hole so sweet you could pour it on your pancakes. Two falls create pools that have to be 25 feet deep and 100 feet wide. An impressive amphitheater of stone with a jumping rock on the left that goes up to about 55 feet. The upper fall doesn't score highly on the usability index. About the only way into and out of this most excellent hole are some slabs down by the lip of the second fall. There are a few seating ledges about 15 feet above the water, but that's limited to no more than a couple of groups. Lots of big, mature black and interior oaks give plenty of shade with nice sunning slabs to the left of them. The best sun is across the shallows at the bottom of the hole on the far bank.

Even though this is dam discharge I have to say water quality is very good. It's deep emerald and quite clear. The water comes from Hetch Hetchy, the reservoir that John Muir tried and failed to prevent. It's ironic that this stretch of river, which is actually outside Yosemite Park, is less disturbed than the Grand Canyon of the Tuolumne which now lies under hundreds of feet of water. Water temperature ranges from pretty damn cold to really damn cold.

Beware of needle litter on the ledges. A fall could take you for a long, injurious ride.

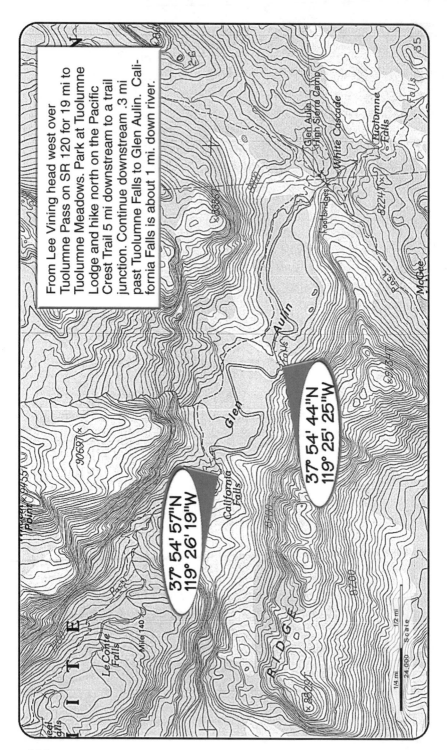

From Lee Vining head west over Tuolumne Pass on SR 120 for 19 mi to Tuolumne Meadows. Park at Tuolumne Lodge and hike north on the Pacific Crest Trail 5 mi downstream to a trail junction. Continue downstream .3 mi past Tuolumne Falls to Glen Aulin. California Falls is about 1 mi. down river.

37° 54' 57"N
119° 26' 19"W

37° 54' 44"N
119° 25' 25"W

Scale
1/4 mi   1/2 mi
24,000

Glen Aulin

The exception to not one, but two rules. Glen Aulin is almost 2,000 vertical feet higher than the average cutoff point for swimming holes included in this book. What's more, there are a couple of man-made structures visible from the water. An inauspicious start, but shoot...no point in being doctrinaire. The prohibition against man-made structures was conceived to ensure that places included here have the appearance of being wild. No swimming holes at dams, next to highways, etc.

Glen Aulin slips by since it's in designated wilderness. Plus it's so pretty. The hole at the bottom is 100 feet wide and 40 to 50 feet long. It's an irregular oval with a fairly small deep end. Not much of a vertical description other than the fall itself, a broken cascade about 40 feet high that slants to the left. Comfortable boulders to sit on, but no slabs for relaxing. Water temp is in the high 50s and the color is that fabulous Yosemite emerald.

Expectation of privacy is zero. Glen Aulin is a popular stopover for backpackers and the site of a High Sierra Camp, one in a series of backcountry lodges that are administered by Yosemite Concession Services. High Sierra Camps require reservations.

part of Northeastern Swimming Holes, a collection of
more than 300 entries from
the Virginias through Maine.

Frenchman's
Fall

California Falls

Looks more like a lagoon than a swimming hole. The deep basin at the lip of California Falls is about 150 feet in diameter, flat and fringed with grass. It looks like prime moose habitat. I spent the entire afternoon waiting there, but alas, no moose. No vertical description at all around the main pool and what would be a tremendous water slide is undone by the sad fact that there's no pool to splash into. The slide terminates into a small tub with a low granite wall and head butting the wall at terminal velocity would take the smile off your face not to mention knocking the teeth out of your mouth.

You'll find good to excellent holes at the lower portion of the falls. Just below the would-be slide is a broad cascade about 40 feet high that comes down into a pool ringed with rectangular boulders. Farther down is another pool that's six feet deep with a *handsome* sand beach—a good lookin' beach—that's located behind a vertical granite slab.

A double diamond day trip based on distance. Most people would want to do this as an overnight. Remember you have to get a wilderness permit even for a day trip and if you stay the night, take a bear canister. Yogi and Booboo want your Powerbars.

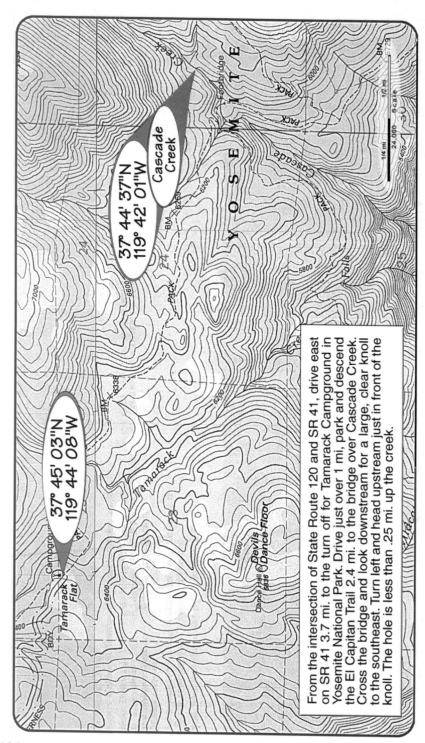

37° 45' 03"N
119° 44' 08"W

37° 44' 37"N
119° 42' 01"W

Cascade Creek

From the intersection of State Route 120 and SR 41, drive east on SR 41 3.7 mi. to the turn off for Tamarack Campground in Yosemite National Park. Drive just over 1 mi, park and descend the El Capitan Trail 2.4 mi. to the bridge over Cascade Creek. Cross the bridge and look downstream for a large, clear knoll to the southeast. Turn left and head upstream just in front of the knoll. The hole is less than .25 mi. up the creek.

Cascade Creek

The very definition of emerald-colored water. So green it's shocking. A slab of granite has fallen flat across the low walls and the effect of this horizontal rock is a little like the arch rock at the El Portal entrance to the park. If you're good at executing shallow dives, this is the place. Although the water immediately below the arch rock is only six feet deep, a headlong dive will put you out toward water eight to ten feet deep. Be advised that this is a small hole and those estimates of depth can vary with the season.

Plenty o' shade combined with sunny ledges. The granite shoulder has several bench seats and bucket seats, some of them so deep and narrow they look like a champagne cooler. The granite is smooth, but with corrugations of just the right size and shape so that your water bottle won't go rolling down the rock into the pool. Water quality is so good, you almost have to call it an excellent hole, but it lacks a great vertical feature.

Even though it's a stone's throw from the popular El Capitan Trail, this hole doesn't seem to get heavily used. Think about visiting after the Tamarack Flat campground is closed in the early part of September. Usership decreases dramatically and, although the road to the campground is closed at the Tioga Road, you can take a mountain bike the two or so miles to the campground.

From Sonora drive south on State Route 49 14.5 mi. to SR 120. Drive east, 68 winding miles, to SR 41 and continue another 19 mi. on SR 120 (Tioga Pass) to parking for Yosemite Creek and the Ten Lakes Trail. Descend on the west side of the creek .75 mi. to a crossing. After crossing, angle west .25 mi. through boulders to a wooded terrace. The pool is below the terrace. Alternately you can approach upstream from the Yosemite Creek Campground, but everything in Yosemite is so congested that entering from above is preferable.

Source: DeLorme Topo

Yosemite
Creek

37° 50' 25"N
119° 35' 05"W

120

Yosemite
Village

41

3 miles
100,000 scale

Yosemite Creek

A perfect equilateral triangle, deep at the apex where the water comes in then it fans out to a shallow wading area at the base of the triangle. Fast water early in the season creates a humdinger of a hole between a pair of rock walls. Then, as the summer wears on, the water warms and settles into the prettiest late season hole you'd ever want to blow bubbles in. It's a good eight to ten feet deep where the water enters and there are modest jumps from the adjoining walls averaging 15 feet or so. Shade abounds on the sandy benches at the bottom and ample sun shines on the ledges. There's even a nice sandy ramp that leads right to the deep end if you want to ease your way in rather than jumping, which may be a good idea because it's trout cold.

Here a late visit is key, early to mid September. Visitorship declines dramatically after the park service closes the Yosemite Creek campground for the season. The trail along Yosemite Creek gets a lot of traffic from backpackers traveling from the valley to the lakes in Tuolumne, but the hole isn't right on the trail so the expectation of privacy is probably good. One note, best approach from above where you can stand on the left-hand headwall and watch the fish and dragon flies before you jump into the gorgeous emerald water and disrupt everything.

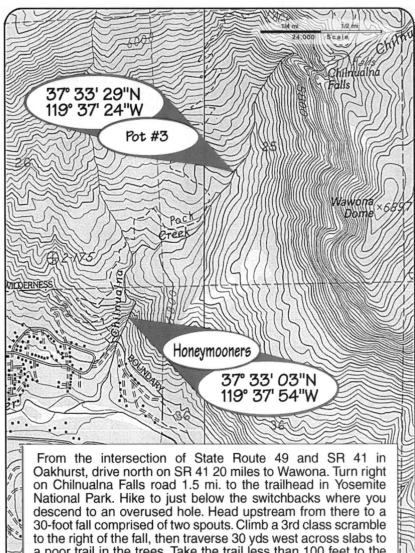

**37° 33' 29"N
119° 37' 24"W**

Pot #3

Chilnualna
Falls

Wawona
Dome ×6897

Pack
Creek

WILDERNESS

BOUNDARY

Honeymooners

**37° 33' 03"N
119° 37' 54"W**

From the intersection of State Route 49 and SR 41 in Oakhurst, drive north on SR 41 20 miles to Wawona. Turn right on Chilnualna Falls road 1.5 mi. to the trailhead in Yosemite National Park. Hike to just below the switchbacks where you descend to an overused hole. Head upstream from there to a 30-foot fall comprised of two spouts. Climb a 3rd class scramble to the right of the fall, then traverse 30 yds west across slabs to a poor trail in the trees. Take the trail less than 100 feet to the top of the ledge.

For Pot #3 return to the main trail and climb the switchbacks to about the 4,900-foot contour where the trail turns northwest. You turn right to the creek and continue less than .25 mi. upstream.

For Chilnualna Falls, return to the main trail and hump it another 1,200 vertical feet up the main trail. At about 6,080 feet descend the granite domes to the east and cross the creek a couple of hundred yards below the falls. Continue upstream on the east bank to the pools.

Honeymooners

Tucked just so, around the corner and up on a ledge, Honeymooners is a darling hideaway pool, just the right size for a couple or small *soiree*. Narrow and smooth, the sides of the pool look like they were poured from concrete. Tremendous sinuous lines with interesting underwater features, submerged bathtubs, ledges, etc. The pool is six to eight feet deep with loads of flat, pink granite surrounding it on the east-west ledge. From this vantage point you see people coming up the creek before they see you, allowing time to, um...collect yourselves.

Also, right before the switchbacks that head up the mountain, are a couple of good to excellent pools. Just upstream from the highly overvisited pool at the bottom of the trail, is a 30-foot falls where two narrow spouts leap over a smooth granite lip into a narrow, cone-shaped pool ten feet deep where privacy is unlikely. Between this fall and Honeymooners is a wide hole that lies along the broad ledge. The 70 foot length of the hole is bounded on one side by a fabulous low-angle slab. The other side is a long ledge, 15 to 20 feet high. Bummer is a big boulder has fallen right into the deep end. So sad.

Privacy is excellent to guaranteed at Honeymooners. Privacy is unlikely at the double fall below as it's much closer to the trail.

Chilnualna Creek

Pot #3

These middle potholes are the *bomb*. They're like hypertrophic Indian bathtubs with vertical sides and smooth geometric contours, but big enough to dive into. Pot #3 is 20 feet long on the major axis and one third as wide. At the bottom is a small basin where you can relax, although shade is scarce. Privacy is good as it's not visible from the trail.

Karen Forest of Palos Verdes has been spending summer vacations at this swimming hole every year for 35 years. "I've got many, many pictures of me and my family at this hole, especially of my daughter. We've been bringing her here every year since she was a baby and now she's a teenager. I don't want to sound corny, but this is a place of spiritual renewal for us."

That's Karen reclining on the rock and her daughter diving into the water on the opposite page. A safety note, it's usually extremely dangerous to dive headlong into a swimming hole. This photo represents a unique case in that, after 35 years of continuous visits, the Forests are aware of submerged obstacles. Plus if mom says it's OK, it usually is.

One note: mosquitoes are numerous and fierce along the Chilnualna Falls Trail. The receding water turns the higher tubs into stagnant pools. Mosquito larvae love it.

Chilnualna Creek

Chilnualna Falls

After a long climb to the top of the granite dome you find a multitiered fall with pools that would be excellent anywhere else. But this is Yosemite and expectations are very high. The pools are ovals, 40 feet on the major axis and scattered with talus that gives them uneven lines. The water is deep enough for some serious swimming, but diving is limited. The canyon faces due west, so even though it's a long hike up, there's enough light to stay late. Expectation of privacy is only fair since the trail, in addition to being a favorite of day hikers, is also used by backpackers going into the high country. The people are, at any rate, more congenial than many visitors found in Yosemite Valley.

Randy Rust, a Park Service fire fighter in Wawona and Yosemite native recalls one corpulent visitor he and a friend had to rescue from the Merced River.

"He came over a little rapid and fell off his tube. He panicked then grabbed onto his son's inner tube and pulled him off too. Me and my friends – we were just kids – we jumped in and dragged him into shallow water. Once he could stand up he starts yelling and sputtering at us."

It seems Rust and his friends, in effecting the rescue, had dislodged the man's dentures. Like good boy scouts, they dived into the river and recovered the choppers from the bottom.

"And you know," Rust said, "he never thanked us for saving his life *or* finding his teeth."

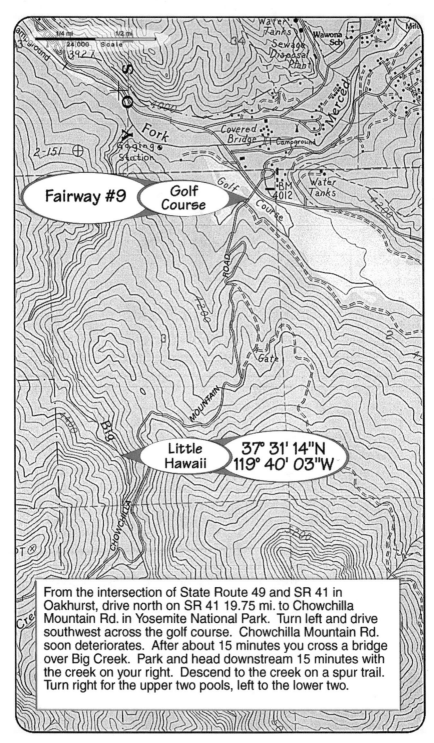

Fairway #9 | Golf Course

Little Hawaii | 37° 31' 14"N 119° 40' 03"W

From the intersection of State Route 49 and SR 41 in Oakhurst, drive north on SR 41 19.75 mi. to Chowchilla Mountain Rd. in Yosemite National Park. Turn left and drive southwest across the golf course. Chowchilla Mountain Rd. soon deteriorates. After about 15 minutes you cross a bridge over Big Creek. Park and head downstream 15 minutes with the creek on your right. Descend to the creek on a spur trail. Turn right for the upper two pools, left to the lower two.

Little Hawaii

Water temperature more alpine than tropical. Little Hawaii is a series of ten or so holes located at the extreme southwest corner of Yosemite Park. The top two holes are the most frequently visited. The first is a broad 15-foot falls that goes into a narrow pool. The second hole is wider, about 45 feet long but with very limited seating on steep slabs with scant shade. Clothing optional.

The middle and lower holes are good for the little dippers. Not as steep or deep and the bottom is sandy. You enter through a short, steep gully, then the best advice is to cross below a large sofa-shaped rock where a sand pocket under some alders to the right makes a nice picnic area. Entry and exit from the water is easier there. Continue downstream about 200 more yards to a second set of three pools. High on the wall you'll find a couple of good-looking bucket seats carved into the granite. Apparently few people visit the lower holes to judge by fact that the most likely exit from the creek was covered with undisturbed detritus. Privacy is excellent down here.

Bonus Feature: You get to drive across the fairway of the Wawona golf course with the prospect of making a well-heeled vacationer fumble his approach shot. Be sure your driver side window is closed, though. Don't want to get a nine iron in the noggin. The fire road may be closed, in which case you'd have to park at the gas station and walk or bike.

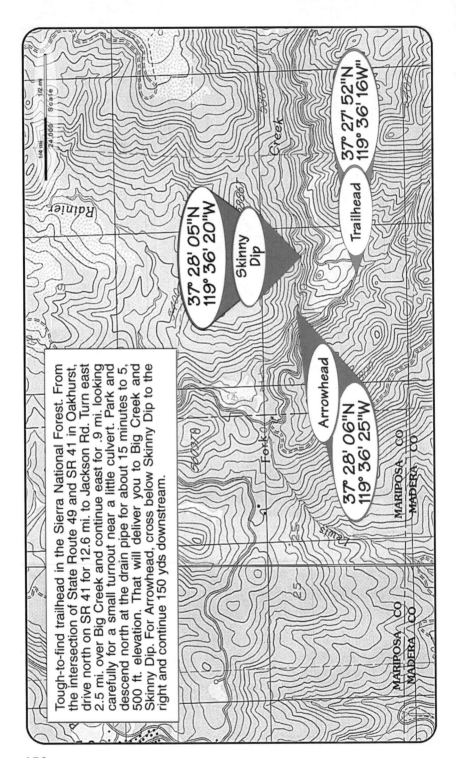

Tough-to-find trailhead in the Sierra National Forest. From the intersection of State Route 49 and SR 41 in Oakhurst, drive north on SR 41 for 12.6 mi. to Jackson Rd. Turn east 2.5 mi. over Big Creek and continue east for .9 mi. looking carefully for a small turnout near a little culvert. Park and descend north at the drain pipe for about 15 minutes to 5,500 ft. elevation. That will deliver you to Big Creek and Skinny Dip. For Arrowhead, cross below Skinny Dip to the right and continue 150 yds downstream.

37° 28' 05"N 119° 36' 20"W

Skinny Dip

37° 27' 52"N 119° 36' 16"W

Trailhead

Arrowhead

37° 28' 06"N 119° 36' 25"W

MARIPOSA CO
MADERA CO

MARIPOSA CO
MADERA CO

Skinny Dip

This is what summer should look like. Toes curling in the water, hands wrapped around a slab of watermelon. Skinny Dip is two sets of falls. The first, a broad cascade, empties into a pool about 60 feet wide and just the right depth for bobbing around and keeping cool on hot August days in the Sierra. The premier feature is the second fall. It dumps 35 feet into a splendiferous container that's distinguished by its impound, a straight-sided lip of granite six feet high that gives the hole the dimensions of a coffee cup. A lounging slab that's maybe 120 sq. ft. occupies the left-hand side between the upper pool and the second fall. There's room for a half dozen people, but beyond that it starts getting crowded. Water temperature is in the mid 60s.

For years Skinny Dip was a secret closely kept by locals, especially Yosemite folk who get tired of summer crowds. Confidentiality was maintained by an extremely difficult-to-find trailhead. Usership has increased recently. Although locals say it's unusual to find 12 people here, it happens. It's around 15 minutes downhill from the turnout. Slabs surrounding the hole are steep for small children, however Labrador retrievers and other water breeds love it here. Note: the name is somewhat misleading; not many people go buff here.

Range cattle stomping through the meadows upstream lower water quality.

Skinny Dip

Arrowhead

This, rather than its upstream brother, should be called Skinny Dip. It's far more private, yet few people seem to go here even when the upper holes are crowded. Shame on them; goody for us. The principal fall is taller than Skinny Dip. Bad news is the hole is only chest high until you get right under the fall. Definitely no diving, but you can just sit at the bottom and dig on the shape of the main pool; it's nearly a perfect arrowhead. Below the main hole are three small, slow pools that average about 30 feet in diameter and are around six feet deep. Gobs of granite to sit on and excellent expectation of privacy. There's good shade away from the main slabs which, in this northwest facing part of the canyon get full sun through the afternoon.

Logging companies built the road past Skinny Dip as a narrow gauge railroad to haul sugar pine trunks down the mountain. Around the same time (1909) the timbermen built a flume to carry logs the rest of the way to the mill. You can inspect the original diversion flume by parking across from the Sugar Pine Road and walking about one mile downhill. There's a fall right at the diversion, but the pool under it is quite shallow.

Bonus Feature: The right hand side of the bank next to the diversion is lined — packed, really — with thimble berries. They're not as juicy as cultivated raspberries, but they have a dynamite flavor, dry and aromatic. Sort of like a raspberry flavored smoke bomb going off in your mouth.

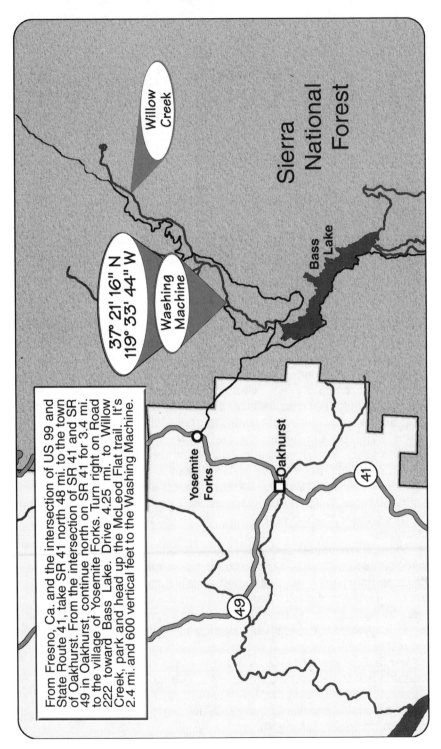

Willow
Creek

Sierra
National
Forest

37° 21' 16" N
119° 33' 44" W

Washing
Machine

Bass
Lake

From Fresno, Ca. and the intersection of US 99 and State Route 41, take SR 41 north 48 mi. to the town of Oakhurst. From the intersection of SR 41 and SR 49 in Oakhurst, continue north on SR 41 for 3.4 mi. to the village of Yosemite Forks. Turn right on Road 222 toward Bass Lake. Drive 4.25 mi. to Willow Creek, park and head up the McLeod Flat trail. It's 2.4 mi. and 600 vertical feet to the Washing Machine.

Yosemite
Forks

Oakhurst

41

49

Washing Machine

Willow Creek looks like the river god went wild with an ice cream scoop, dipping big round balls of granite out of the bed rock. Washing Machine gets its name from a series of three smallish potholes connected by submerged passageways. You jump into the top one, a coffin-sized rock vault that's so deeply excavated and enclosed it almost has a roof. You pop through a hole in the side to a smaller tub with churning water. Deep in that pot you'll find another passage that puts you out into a third tub which discharges through a passage onto a short rock ramp that delivers you – grinning broadly– into the main pool. Ample seating on the slabs and lots of space which may be required since this hole is widely known among locals.

There are several other popular swimming holes along the creek: Angel Falls and Devil's Slide to name a couple. The Slide, were it reviewed separately, would be rated a double diamond because this is a big, dangerous fall that's killed several people. The creek between Devil's and Washing Machine is more user friendly. It looks like the moon, it has so many craters—as many as 500, ranging in size from kiddie pools to big Roman baths.

Bass Lake residents take their drinking water from Willow Creek. They've been doing it so long the riveted steel pipes carrying the water to the chlorinating facility are shot full of leaks down below Angel Falls. It's kind of fun to walk along the pipe and watch water leaping 20 feet into the air at each pipe joint.

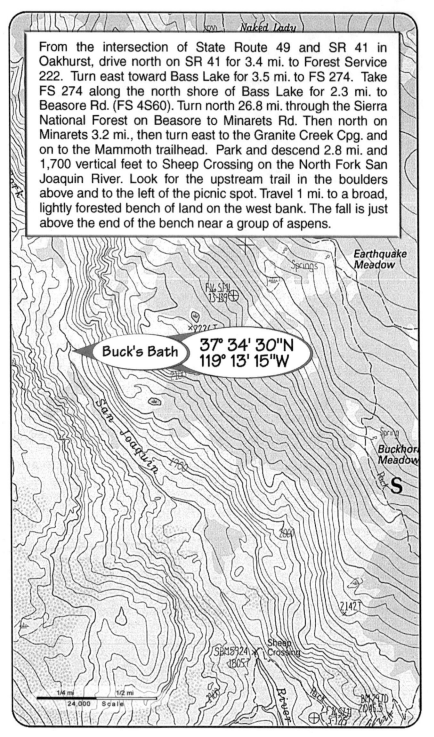

From the intersection of State Route 49 and SR 41 in Oakhurst, drive north on SR 41 for 3.4 mi. to Forest Service 222. Turn east toward Bass Lake for 3.5 mi. to FS 274. Take FS 274 along the north shore of Bass Lake for 2.3 mi. to Beasore Rd. (FS 4S60). Turn north 26.8 mi. through the Sierra National Forest on Beasore to Minarets Rd. Then north on Minarets 3.2 mi., then turn east to the Granite Creek Cpg. and on to the Mammoth trailhead. Park and descend 2.8 mi. and 1,700 vertical feet to Sheep Crossing on the North Fork San Joaquin River. Look for the upstream trail in the boulders above and to the left of the picnic spot. Travel 1 mi. to a broad, lightly forested bench of land on the west bank. The fall is just above the end of the bench near a group of aspens.

Naked Lady

Earthquake Meadow

Springs

Buck's Bath 37° 34' 30"N 119° 13' 15"W

San Joaquin

Spring

Buckhor Meadow

S

Sheep Crossing

1/4 mi   1/2 mi
24,000   Scale

Buck's Bath

Buck's Bath sits right on the lower edge of aspen habitat at the head of a long, wide bench of land that's covered with a really, really nice conifer parkland. Ponderosa and sugar pine trees are widely spaced, letting dappled light fall on the biggest, flattest picnic area you ever saw. Seriously, it's the size of an RV park and it's right next to this dyno pool. The hole is eight to ten feet deep and cobble lined. Walls are 30 to 45 feet high, some of them overhanging. Ample slabs above the hole provide plenty of space for relaxing and catching rays. When you get hot you can slip over the lip and into the cold water. And it *is* cold – high 50s in August. The fall is tucked around a corner and it's actually difficult to see.

The seclusion helps explain why the fall doesn't have a name. In fact, fewer than half of the swimming holes I found have agreed-upon names. I either make one up or invite local folks to name them. This swimming hole is named for Buck Tyree, a Korea vet and modern day mountain man who, local guide Jay Ericson says, lives in the canyons below Sheep Crossing.

"He's got all sorts of hidden camps up and down the canyons. I've never seen him," Ericson concedes, "but people sometimes pick him and his dog up hitchhiking."

So if you're in the area and you meet a guy with a limp and a dog called Boots, tell him somebody named a swimming hole after him.

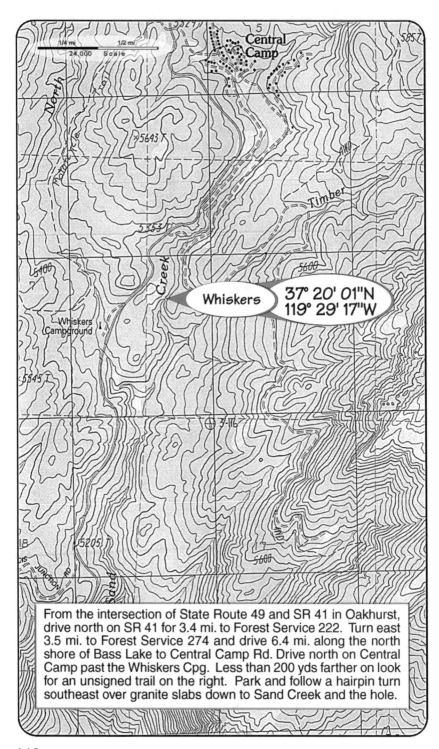

Whiskers

37° 20' 01"N
119° 29' 17"W

From the intersection of State Route 49 and SR 41 in Oakhurst, drive north on SR 41 for 3.4 mi. to Forest Service 222. Turn east 3.5 mi. to Forest Service 274 and drive 6.4 mi. along the north shore of Bass Lake to Central Camp Rd. Drive north on Central Camp past the Whiskers Cpg. Less than 200 yds farther on look for an unsigned trail on the right. Park and follow a hairpin turn southeast over granite slabs down to Sand Creek and the hole.

Whiskers

FAIR

Possibly the most kid friendly swimming hole in this book. Broad, low-angle slabs keep baby from tipping over and rolling down the mountain. There are five tubs, each four to five feet deep. Small tubs give little ones something that looks so much like the bath at home that they'll be bummed there's no bubbly shampoo. Actually, the holes here aren't really big enough or deep enough to be reviewed were it not for the access they offer families with young children. Although easy to get to, there's very little litter. Unlimited seating and a potentially a cool mountain bike ride. Southern Yosemite Mountain Guides, a Bass Lake outfitter, often takes bike tours up Central Camp Road to Whiskers.

Whiskers allegedly gets its name from the Mono Indians who used rock above the swimming hole as grinding stones. While they were working on the acorns they'd be surreptitiously watched by mountain lions hiding off to the side of the swimming hole. According to legend, the only way the Indians could detect the cats was to catch a glimpse of the animal's long whiskers. It's difficult to tell if that's a factual story, however the part about the grinding stones is true. You can see the holes worked into the rock.

Why Bother

Natural Bridges

Natural Bridges isn't simply down in a canyon, it's underground. The small creek has bored two large tubes through the limestone. Water quality is poor and the place is overrun with air mattresses and pool toys.

Devil's Slide

Marvelously steep, but too many injuries.

Lower Willow Creek

Litter includes adhesive bandages, cigarette butts and, on one day, hair trimmings from a little boy who was reluctantly shorn during a slow point in the summer fun.

Granite Creek

Chest deep and right next to a campground.

Big Pool

High school party spot near Readington Reservoir.

Cascadel

A really pretty falls, but it's a neighborhood spot that's closely shared by the residents of Cascadel Woods and Cascadel Heights and what the heck—there are more than enough places to go in the Sierra without intruding.

Yosemite Creek Falls Trail

Nice pool at the top of the famed falls, but do you really want to spend your time outdoors rubbing shoulders with 40 to 50 strangers?

Rainbow Pool

On the South Fork Tuolumne. Crowds.

The Sequoias &
Southern Sierra

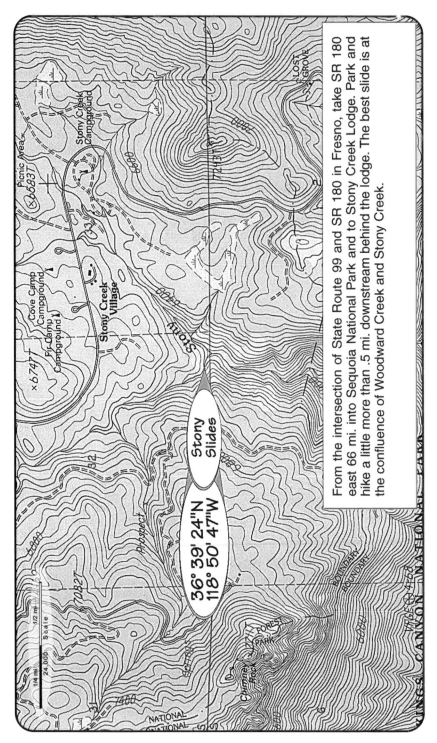

From the intersection of State Route 99 and SR 180 in Fresno, take SR 180 east 66 mi. into Sequoia National Park and to Stony Creek Lodge. Park and hike a little more than .5 mi. downstream behind the lodge. The best slide is at the confluence of Woodward Creek and Stony Creek.

Stony Slides

36° 39' 24"N
118° 50' 47"W

Stony Slides

A pair of water slides that will keep the kids busy for hours. Not really any place to swim, though. Just slide, splash. Repeat. The upper chute, the longer of the two at about 40 feet, is especially suited for the little dippers. It's narrow with half-dozen woopty do's terminating in a small, deep pool. The chute seems carved for kids, just wide enough for juvenile hips, but a little narrow for more ample backsides. The lower slide is a little shorter. The course isn't as defined and the pool at the bottom isn't as deep, either. But the cool thing is the dappled appearance of the surrounding rock.

Most of it is granodiorite. Nothing exotic about that, much of the Sierra is granodiorite. But within the rock are some dark stones called enclaves that have been worn smooth by the water until they look like carefully laid paving stones. There are a couple of theories on how this happened. One is that the granite magma scooped up unmelted mantle. Alternately some hypothesize that the magma enveloped loose rocks on its trip to the surface.

You will not be alone. Alder Slabs is among the most popular swimming holes in the Sequoia. That's because, although it's a long drive, the hike is suitable for the youngest family members. Litter is not as bad as it might be; however, there's some broken glass. Range cattle diminish water quality.

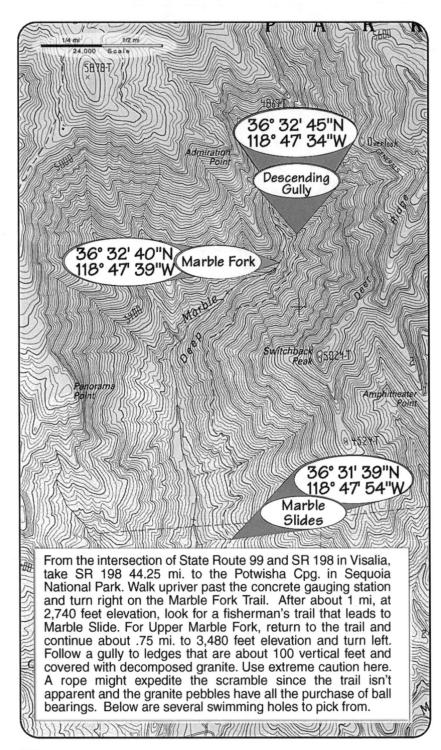

36° 32' 45"N
118° 47' 34"W

Descending Gully

36° 32' 40"N
118° 47' 39"W

Marble Fork

36° 31' 39"N
118° 47' 54"W

Marble Slides

From the intersection of State Route 99 and SR 198 in Visalia, take SR 198 44.25 mi. to the Potwisha Cpg. in Sequoia National Park. Walk upriver past the concrete gauging station and turn right on the Marble Fork Trail. After about 1 mi, at 2,740 feet elevation, look for a fisherman's trail that leads to Marble Slide. For Upper Marble Fork, return to the trail and continue about .75 mi. to 3,480 feet elevation and turn left. Follow a gully to ledges that are about 100 vertical feet and covered with decomposed granite. Use extreme caution here. A rope might expedite the scramble since the trail isn't apparent and the granite pebbles have all the purchase of ball bearings. Below are several swimming holes to pick from.

Marble Fork

Turn your back on the crowds and open your arms to one of the finest swimming rivers in the state. As many as one dozen pools and holes are connected by creamy waterfalls stacked one on top of the other like a gargantuan wedding cake. The best part is you get a stunning overview of all the falls shortly before turning down the descent.

The tallest is about 60 feet high and lies roughly in the middle of the wedding cake. Upstream are four excellent holes, a couple of which require some third class scrambling to reach. The first is a broad, 25-foot-tall torrent from which you can jump into a 12-foot-deep bowl of water. Some of the slabs are well situated for relaxation. Ditto the next pool. The left side is all low-angle slabs optimally aligned for summer repose. The pool is not as deep as the first and it has few jumps, but at 80 feet long it's twice as large. Above that are two more pools, the uppermost with abundant fuscias growing around it.

The river faces southwest and a tall north-south ridge means best sun is noon to 3 p.m. Water quality is good, but sphincter shutting cold. Lots of plant glop, but that together with the overgrown and lightly compacted trail suggests few people swim here. Privacy is just about guaranteed.

Marble Fork

Marble Slide

Don't feel like hoofing it all the way up to the double diamond falls? Lower down on the Marble Fork are a couple of excellent holes and one of the best siesta beaches you're likely to find. It's a beautiful sand pocket interspersed with cobbles and it hosts a fully grown live oak tree with high branches you don't have to crouch to get under for shade. Granite walls loom 35 feet above the water. Really comfortable to sit on and get some sun there; not especially easy to get down to the water and, at just six feet deep, jumping in from the slabs is out of the question. Just above is what appears to be a rootin' tootin' rip-roaring hootenanny of a water slide.

But is any of this legal? A park ranger told me that it's against the law to swim in any of the rivers of Sequoia National Park. There is at least one drowning per summer from idiots who jump in the roaring Kings River which dispatches them with Darwinian swiftness. It's sensible to restrict people from dangerous waterways, but a blanket prohibition against swimming seemed overly broad. So I asked to see the statute, at which point the ranger started stammering that all the law enforcement rangers were out of the office and he couldn't find the regulation book. Yeah, right. A call to the park headquarters indicated there is no such law. So go ahead and jump in; just use good sense.

Privacy is excellent-to-guaranteed at Marble Slide to judge by the lightly used trail.

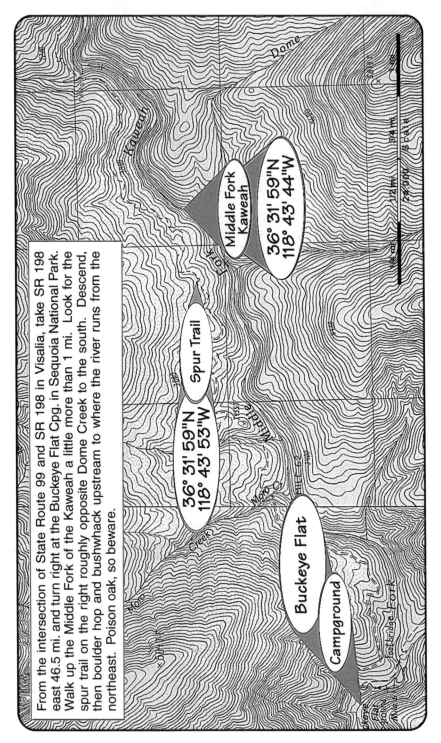

From the intersection of State Route 99 and SR 198 in Visalia, take SR 198 east 46.5 mi. and turn right at the Buckeye Flat Cpg. in Sequoia National Park. Walk up the Middle Fork of the Kaweah a little more than 1 mi. Look for the spur trail on the right roughly opposite Dome Creek to the south. Descend, then boulder hop and bushwhack upstream to where the river runs from the northeast. Poison oak, so beware.

36° 31' 59"N
118° 43' 53"W

Spur Trail

36° 31' 59"N
118° 43' 44"W

Middle Fork Kaweah

Buckeye Flat

Campground

Middle Fork Kaweah

Hurry. Sometime during the coming century a huge boulder poised on the right bank will probably dump into the deep end, making a wading spot out of what is now a deep, deep bowl. Unlike many holes that are only really deep at the bottom of the fall, this one is bodacious throughout. Only thing that prevents this from being a classic is the lack of any overwhelming vertical element like a tall fall or pendulous rock formation. Waterslide potential for the brave and a couple of fair jumps, the best one being a 35-footer off the top of the right hand boulder, the one that's poised to fall into the middle of the hole. Commodious water-polished slabs, some with butt buckets carved in them for luxury seating.

Located at the bottom of a granite constriction, this is one of several fabulous holes on the Middle Fork of the Kaweah. Problem is the lower ones are within sight of a road or power lines (this one is barely around the corner from such engineered intrusions) and the upper ones are just plain inaccessible without a chainsaw and power scythe. Even the short hike to this spot requires moderate bush-whacking. Near as I can tell this spot is very lightly visited. I judge privacy as excellent to guaranteed. River runs northeast to south, so this is a good place to get out of the late afternoon sun.

From the intersection of State Route 99 and SR 198 in Visalia, take SR 198 ito the hills for 34.5 mi. to South Fork Road. Turn right and drive 6.4 mi. to the South Fork Cpg. Walk east a short distance and cross to the north bank of the river. Continue east up a jeep trail for less than .5 mi. to a small, usually dry creek. After the creek, climb a short hill (10 vertical feet) and start looking for the spur trail on your right. Descend a short distance to the river bed and brush bust your way a couple of thousand feet upstream.

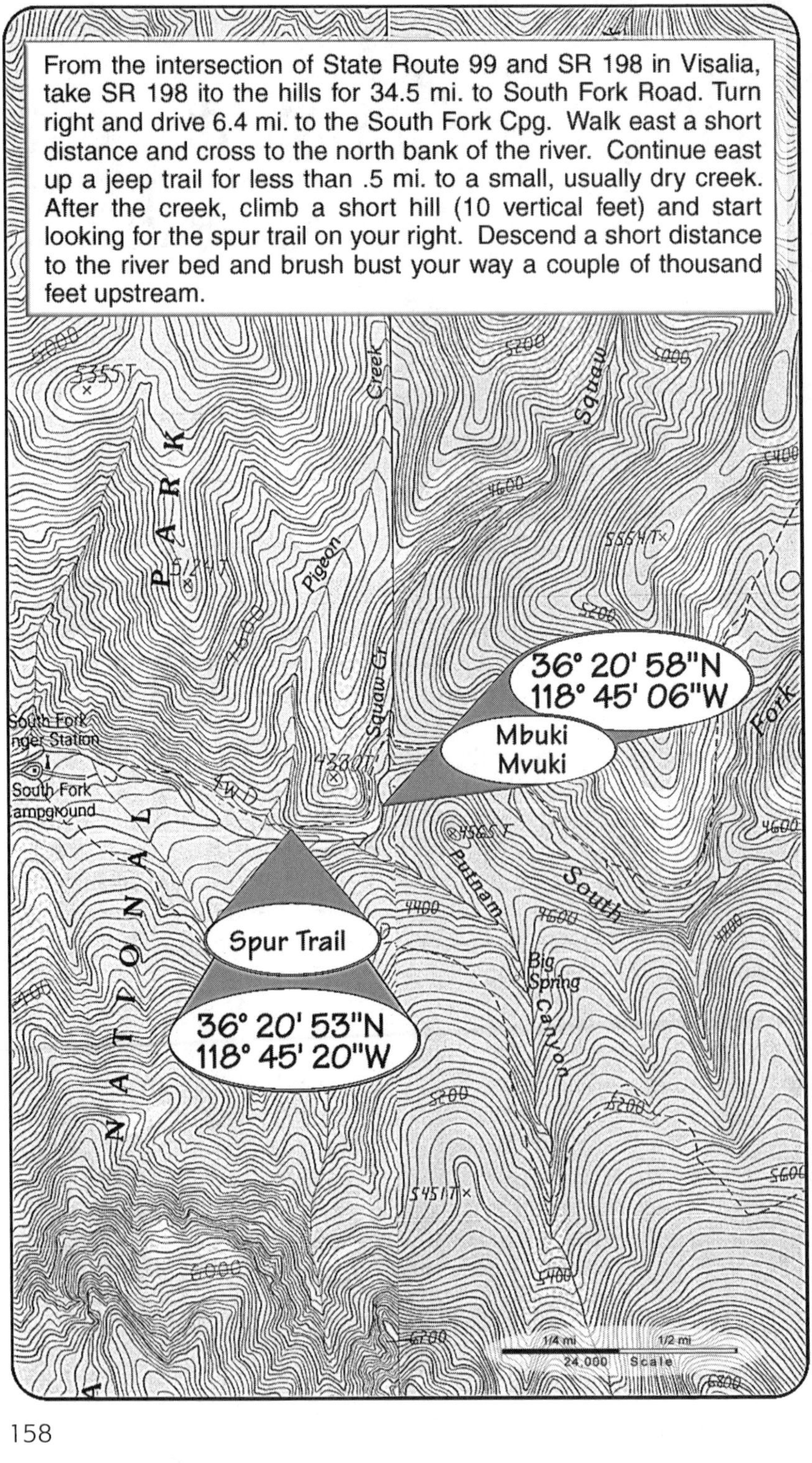

36° 20' 58"N
118° 45' 06"W

Mbuki
Mvuki

Spur Trail

36° 20' 53"N
118° 45' 20"W

Mbuki
Mvuki

Pronounced em-BO-ki em-VO-ki. The name comes from a Bantu verb meaning "to shuck off one's clothes." This is the place to go on a too sunny day. Shallow pools and deep shade that, together with the brisk waters of the Kaweah River, will keep you cool when the surrounding vegetation is at flash point. Both pools are at the bottom of short cascades, each cascade about six feet tall and twice as long. Both are ovals measuring about 20 feet on the major axis and about eight feet deep under the cascades. Kind of shallow and bouldery on the downstream end, though. Alders among the boulders give deep shade, but the rocks are too tightly grouped for anything like a picnic area. Best place to cool it is a flat rock finger that divides one of the pools in half. Dandy spot in a little-visited corner of the park where buckeye, live oak and Douglas fir out-populate giant seqoias. The expectation of privacy is excellent.

The South Fork of the Kaweah was the scene of a dramatic geologic event not too long ago, at least not long ago geologically speaking. In 1867 it rained and snowed for 41 days. On Dec. 20 the north side of Dennison Mountain broke away and several hundred acres of land crashed into the South Fork. Sequoias from the Garfield Grove, many 20 to 30-feet in diameter, formed a dam 400 feet tall. The obstruction lasted about 24 hours before it burst and sent millions of tons of debris spreading for miles across the Central Valley around Visalia.

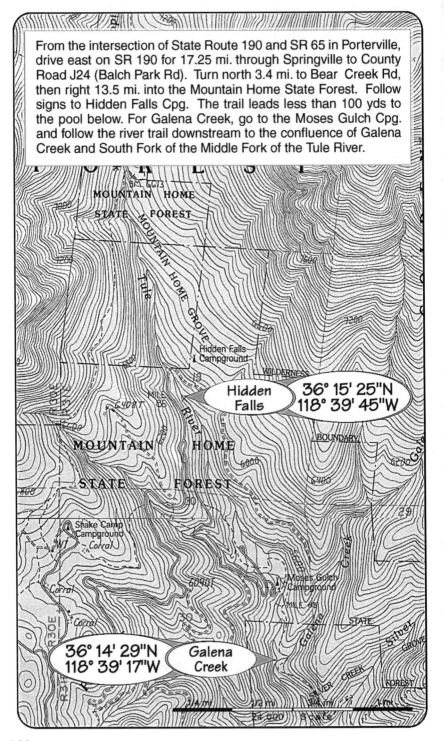

From the intersection of State Route 190 and SR 65 in Porterville, drive east on SR 190 for 17.25 mi. through Springville to County Road J24 (Balch Park Rd). Turn north 3.4 mi. to Bear Creek Rd, then right 13.5 mi. into the Mountain Home State Forest. Follow signs to Hidden Falls Cpg. The trail leads less than 100 yds to the pool below. For Galena Creek, go to the Moses Gulch Cpg. and follow the river trail downstream to the confluence of Galena Creek and South Fork of the Middle Fork of the Tule River.

Hidden Falls 36° 15' 25"N 118° 39' 45"W

36° 14' 29"N 118° 39' 17"W Galena Creek

Hidden Falls

A schist chute fills a fan-shaped pool. Both shoulders of the pool are vertical rock, the faces near mirror images of one another. A nice, symmetric look to be sure, but the pool is shallow because there's no impound, just a load of cobble at the end of the pool. Well-meaning visitors stacked more stones at the discharge, thereby raising the water one inch – maybe. The ragged little line of rocks reduces the sense of wilderness and normally any man-made structure will disqualify a swimming hole, but I let this one go because the adjoining campground is so enchanting.

It's a walk-in and extremely quiet, set as it is on a riverside terrace under a canopy of sequoias. Hundreds of bracken ferns fill the area between sequoia trunks, creating a remarkable space that's filled with flat, shadowy light tinted by the high tree tops. Once inside, people speak at a whisper.

The river faces south. Midday sun is good and the southern exposure means a longer season. Little privacy, though, as the falls are less that one-quarter mile from the road.

Galena Creek

Galena Creek

A pool so narrow, you have to go on a diet to get in. Both the river and the creek that runs into it spill over ledges. Like much of the schist bed in the upper Tule, the rock is aligned at a right angle to the water flow so the river chisels a narrow chute in the rock. The steep sides are surrounded on 180 degrees by cascading water. Lots of shade from the adjoining sequoias. Ferns and penstemons complete the frame on this tiny, precious container of water that's less than half as wide as the trees surrounding it.

The giant sequoias of the Mountain Home State Forest escaped the sawyers until 1944 when the owners of the private forest began falling the trees. The state stepped in and bought the land to preserve it. Some logging still goes on though. Salvage loggers dissect door-sized slabs from trunks toppled by natural causes. Oddly enough, redwood seems only to turn red when exposed. Look at a pile of fresh sawdust and it has the characteristic rusty pink color on top, but drag a toe through it and you'll discover the unexposed sawdust has an ordinary color.

Downstream from Galena Creek you'll find another pool, oblanceolate in shape and, at eight feet, slightly deeper than the pool above. Ample rock ledges to lie on and a fair expectation of privacy, although the pool is visible from the trail traveling north.

From the intersection of State Route 190 and SR 65 in Porterville, drive east on SR 190 through the town of Springville and into Sequoia National Forest. Continue east on SR 190 for a total of 25.8 mi. from Porterville. Look for a turnout on the south side of the road. That's the Stevenson Trail. Descend to the South Fork of the Tule River. There's one over used hole at the bottom of the trail and another less molested one about 100 yds farther up.

36° 09' 35"N
118° 41' 14"W

Parking

Stevenson Gully

36° 09' 30"N
118° 41' 02"W

Stevenson Gully

Radiant water. It's a pale, mineral green filing a triangular pool with a cattail and peppermint fringe at the hem. The water quality is so good you can see clear to the bottom and it's 12 feet at least. The bottom is smooth and even. Ledges are ample, but the shade is limited. Jumps are 15 and 20 feet.

The Middle Fork of the Tule River is a watershed that, were it not for the rude intrusion of roads, would be salted with mega classics. The road up to Camp Wishon is loaded, just loaded, with great swimming holes. But they're so easily accessible that the river is swamped by the boom box brigades. Hwy 190 between Coffee Creek and Camp Nelson is not quite as exposed, but still there are a couple of holes visible from the road and they evidently suffer from punks and yahoos.

Stevenson is barely more than a stone's throw from the highway, although the road isn't visible from the fall. It's further protected by the fact that there's a heavily used hole right at the bottom of the spur trail that attracts the monster truck crowd and prevents them from wandering upstream where the peppermint starts. Privacy is not to be had on a weekend. Try a weekday visit.

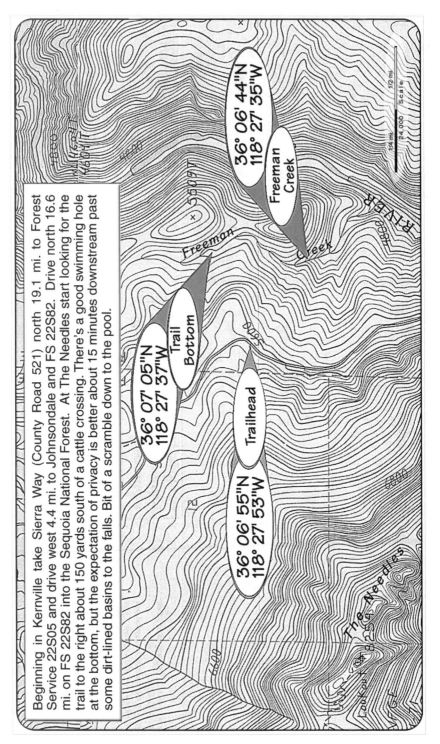

Beginning in Kernville take Sierra Way (County Road 521) north 19.1 mi. to Forest Service 22S05 and drive west 4.4 mi. to Johnsondale and FS 22S82. Drive north 16.6 mi. on FS 22S82 into the Sequoia National Forest. At The Needles start looking for the trail to the right about 150 yards south of a cattle crossing. There's a good swimming hole at the bottom, but the expectation of privacy is better about 15 minutes downstream past some dirt-lined basins to the falls. Bit of a scramble down to the pool.

36° 06' 44"N
118° 27' 35"W

Freeman Creek

Creek

Freeman

36° 07' 05"N
118° 27' 37"W

Trail Bottom

36° 06' 55"N
118° 27' 53"W

Trailhead

The Needles

RIVER

1/4 mi.   1/2 mi.
24,000   Scale

Freeman Creek

Privacy. Once you find the trailhead it's a 15-minute, bushwhacking descent, then another 15 minutes or so downstream to an 80-foot fall. At the bottom is a smooth geometric pool 10 feet wide, 30 feet long, but barely six feet deep due to the decomposed granite filling the bottom. There's also a good tub at the top of the falls where water has cut a pretty alcove into the granite shoulder of the stream bed. Off to the west you can clearly see The Needles, a collection of granite spires that attracts rock climbers from around the world.

Pete Brewer grew up on the other side of The Needles helping his dad at the family's restaurant and bar, the Ponderosa Lodge. As a boy he'd troll the bottom of swimming holes for stuff people left behind.

"I found rings, bracelets, all sorts of jewelry, wallets and two guns." One was a Ruger .22-cal. revolver he found half-buried with the muzzle sticking up out of the sand. "I figure the guy had it in a hip holster and when he hopped over a rock it popped out without him realizing it. At the time the county had a 25-cent bounty on ground squirrels. Bring in a tail, you get a quarter. Let me tell you, 13 years old with that little Ruger, I was the bounty hunter de lux."

High water, not loaded handguns, is the big danger here. Water is turbid. Decomposing plant matter in some dirt-lined basins above the falls may be to blame.

Alder Slabs

36° 02' 13"N
118° 31' 01"W

36° 01' 38"N
118° 30' 49"W

Camp 4

36° 01' 10"N
118° 30' 49"W

Parking

Beginning in Kernville, take Sierra Way (County Road 521) north 14.1 mi. to Forest Service 22S05 and drive west 4.4 mi. to FS 22S82 in Johnsondale. Turn north 5.4 mi. through the Sequoia National Forest to a roadside pullout on the right, parking for Camp 4. To reach Alder Slabs continue north on FS 22S82 for .8 mi. to FS 22S83. The road is gated, so park without blocking the gate and walk north about .75 mi. to a point just above where Alder Creek enters Dry Meadow Creek.

Camp 4

The place to do your summer reading. The potholes are nice enough, but the most engaging features are the slabs — vast expanses of smooth rock, nearly level and broadly shaded by Jeffrey Pines. If you could get the Sunday New York Times delivered, it would be perfect. Anyway, back to the swimming hole. The fall is a tier stacked around a narrow, winding chute. The two holes at the bottom are tight, about 20 feet in diameter and six to eight feet deep. The rock bed is probably a good deal deeper, but it has been filled in with decomposed granite. Because it's difficult to get out of the water, someone placed a steel hook in the granite above the first hole, presumably for attaching a rope so you can hand over hand back out. There's also a haul out between the two pools.

A warning: many blackflies. They breed in clear, fast moving water so they are ubiquitous at swimming holes. The average black fly doesn't respect personal space. People I've talked to are divided on which black flies are worse: ones that fly in your mouth or ones that fly in your ear. I say ear. The potential for getting an angry fly stuck against your ear drum is way more daunting than spitting out a tiny bit of bug.

Expectation of privacy is poor as the holes are a short walk from a drive-up campground.

Brush Creek

Alder Slabs

A pair of water slides that will keep the kids busy for hours. Not really any place to swim, though. Just slide, splash. Repeat. The upper chute, the longer of the two at about 40 feet, is especially suited for the little dippers. It's narrow with half-dozen woopty do's terminating in a small, deep pool. The chute seems carved for kids, just wide enough for juvenile hips, but a little narrow for more ample backsides. The lower slide is a little shorter. The course isn't as defined and the pool at the bottom isn't as deep, either. But the cool thing is the dappled appearance of the surrounding rock.

Most of it is granodiorite. Nothing exotic about that, much of the Sierra is granodiorite. But within the rock are some dark stones called enclaves that have been worn smooth by the water until they look like carefully laid paving stones. There are a couple of theories on how this happened. One is that the granite magma scooped up unmelted mantle. Alternately some hypothesize that the magma enveloped loose rocks on its trip to the surface.

You will not be alone. Alder Slabs is among the most popular swimming holes in the Sequoia. That's because, although it's a long drive, the hike is suitable for the youngest family members. Litter is not as bad as it might be; however, there's some broken glass. Range cattle diminish water quality.

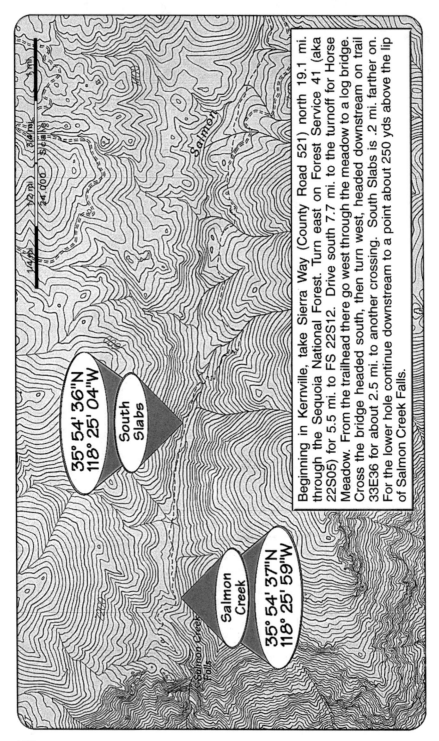

Beginning in Kernville, take Sierra Way (County Road 521) north 19.1 mi. through the Sequoia National Forest. Turn east on Forest Service 41 (aka 22S05) for 5.5 mi. to FS 22S12. Drive south 7.7 mi. to the turnoff for Horse Meadow. From the trailhead there go west through the meadow to a log bridge. Cross the bridge headed south, then turn west, headed downstream on trail 33E36 for about 2.5 mi. to another crossing. South Slabs is .2 mi. farther on. For the lower hole continue downstream to a point about 250 yds above the lip of Salmon Creek Falls.

35° 54' 36"N
118° 25' 04"W

South Slabs

Salmon Creek

35° 54' 37"N
118° 25' 59"W

South
Slabs

A small pool deeply recessed 100 feet below decomposing slabs. You'd expect the "DG" would fill in much of the tub. Instead the water is eight to 10 feet deep with a smooth, even bottom, unobstructed by talus. You can even dive into it from a yard-high granite platform on the downstream side. On the left bank are commodious slabs that face due south. They're set at a brilliant angle for relaxation and sunning. If you start to grill, there's adequate, though not luxurious, shade farther up on the slab near the trees or downstream on leaf litter and duff among still more trees.

The only bad thing to say about Salmon Creek is cattle upstream have damaged the riparian habitat and may be diminishing water quality. Officials have fenced off the creek to cattle and have started a program to monitor the water for nitrates and fecal coliform. So far no cause for alarm and experts say that the threat of contamination is reduced during the summer swimming season since the area experiences few rain showers that would wash cow manure into the stream.

The trail isn't that great in spots. Since you're following the drainage off the Kern Plateau, you can't get lost. You may, however, have trouble finding the most expedient path to get where you want to go. Privacy is excellent.

Bull Run

Salmon Creek

Awesome place to take a date. Three lobes of water separated by a septum of polished granite. Water free falls into a six-foot-deep pool—a very sharp pool, even though sand deposits in the bottom limit the depth. Good news is the sediment is presumably grinding deeper into the bedrock. In a few thousand years this could be the place to visit. While you're waiting, you and your significant other can loll under the intimacy of a white fir bower that's fitted over a slab above and to the left of the falls.

No trip to Salmon Creek would be complete without visiting Salmon Creek Falls. Most people only get a distant peek at the falls from the South Rincon Trail below. From the top, the views of the Kern Canyon and Western Divide are expansive. It's no more than a couple of hundred yards from the pools down to the point where the creek exits the Kern Plateau and accelerates toward Lake Isabella and the thirsty irrigation pipes of the Central Valley. The falls themselves are breathtaking, but getting to the bottom is a major technical undertaking. There was once a trail, but these days trying to reach the bottom isn't at all recommended.

Bring a field guide, a fishing pole or both. You may be lucky enough to find some trout hiding in the creek and Kern ceanothus, larkspur, monkshood and lupine standing out boldly on the hills above it.

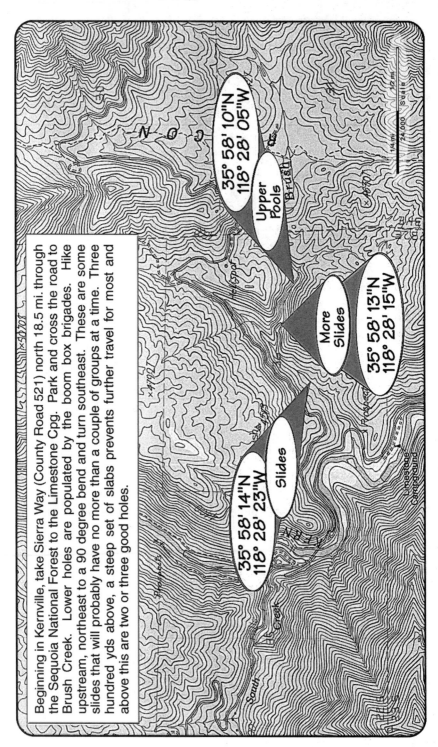

Beginning in Kernville, take Sierra Way (County Road 521) north 18.5 mi. through the Sequoia National Forest to the Limestone Cpg. Park and cross the road to Brush Creek. Lower holes are populated by the boom box brigades. Hike upstream, northeast to a 90 degree bend and turn southeast. These are some slides that will probably have no more than a couple of groups at a time. Three hundred yds above, a steep set of slabs prevents further travel for most and above this are two or three good holes.

Upper Pools
35° 58' 10"N
118° 28' 05"W

More Slides
35° 58' 13"N
118° 28' 15"W

Slides
35° 58' 14"N
118° 28' 23"W

Scale 1:24,000

Brush Creek

A string of pearls draped over the left shoulder of the Kern. Brush Creek contains more than one dozen swimmable holes in the three miles between the highway and top of the canyon. The lower ones are way too heavily visited. It's a little less rowdy at the main cascade, which is about 45 feet long. Not much to jump off, but there's a killer water slide. Above that the canyon opens up to broad slabs, about 300 feet wide at a southeast to southwest bend in the river where you'll find a similar, though smaller, waterslide.

The crowds don't thin out 'til after some steep slabs. Above the slabs is a 60-foot pool that's open and sunny with a rim that's 500 feet across at the top. Depth of the water is not that great, six to eight feet deep. Limited shade. Better pools farther up where the water comes into a granite hole 20 feet across with sheer-sided walls rising 100 feet or so. The fall cascades over a bulge in the rock, falling free for about ten feet. Excellent expectation of privacy.

The best Brush Creek has to offer is farther still, through a small but thick stand of alder and willow. It's a nice little honeymooner's tub and a couple of pools, the uppermost has a 100 square feet of slab to sit on. Almost certainly the most secluded pool on the creek. Farther up the creek flattens out.

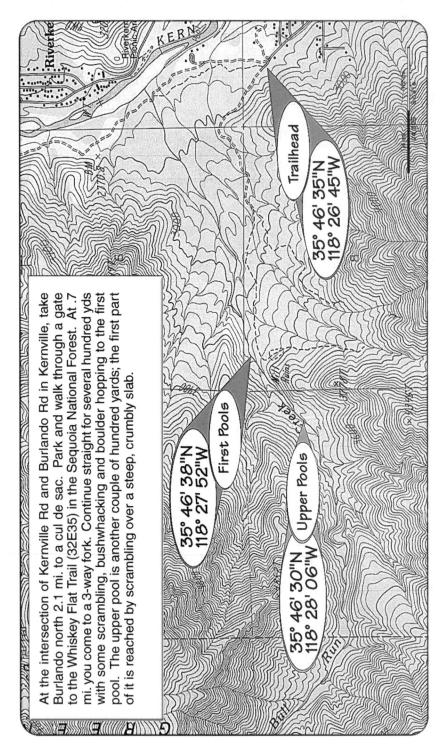

At the intersection of Kernville Rd and Burlando Rd in Kernville, take Burlando north 2.1 mi. to a cul de sac. Park and walk through a gate to the Whiskey Flat Trail (32E35) in the Sequoia National Forest. At .7 mi. you come to a 3-way fork. Continue straight for several hundred yds with some scrambling, bushwhacking and boulder hopping to the first pool. The upper pool is another couple of hundred yards; the first part of it is reached by scrambling over a steep, crumbly slab.

Trailhead
35° 46' 35"N
118° 26' 45"W

First Pools
35° 46' 38"N
118° 27' 52"W

Upper Pools
35° 46' 30"N
118° 28' 06"W

Bull Run Creek

A combo platter with four pools and several falls. Here's the rundown: The uppermost pool lies at the bottom of a triple falls. The second pool is fed by a double falls, the third functions as catch for a good-looking waterslide. The lowest—and most swimmable pool—lies under a short, notch falls. Most of the pools are not much more than six feet deep, good but not excellent. They are, however, beautiful to look at. The third is the most photogenic. In addition to the slide above it, the pool is fringed with alders, cattails and a host of other water-loving species. The unfortunate aspect of this is there's lots of plant goo. Kick around much and the water starts to look like tea and milk. All of the holes are good with ample seating, but not much to jump from.

This area used to be much less placid. A nearby smelter served a number of local mines as late as the early 1900s. Huts, tailing ponds and trash piles pocked the landscape. About one mile into the trail you come to a three-way split. The left trail leads to the smelter ruins and unmortared stones laid down parallel to one another. Most of the rest of the structure has been carried away.

The trail up to the pools is unmaintained and lightly trodden. You can get by with just sandals, but running shoes are recommended. Expectation of privacy is good; however, I did find some litter.

Why Bother

Nobe Young
Pretty little falls, but hardly more than hip deep.

Coffee Camp
Beat and overrun.

Boulder Creek
Beat and overrun, the sequel.

Peppermint Falls
Stunning falls, but not swimmable. So sad.

Hospital Rock
Hard by the campgrounds. Too many people.

Indian Head
Road visible above river.

Silver Creek
Fireroad leads down to an abandoned copper mine. Four-wheel drives and lots of litter.

Wishon
Pretty water all along North Fork of Tule, but power lines, graffiti and trash.

Santa Barbara & Ojai

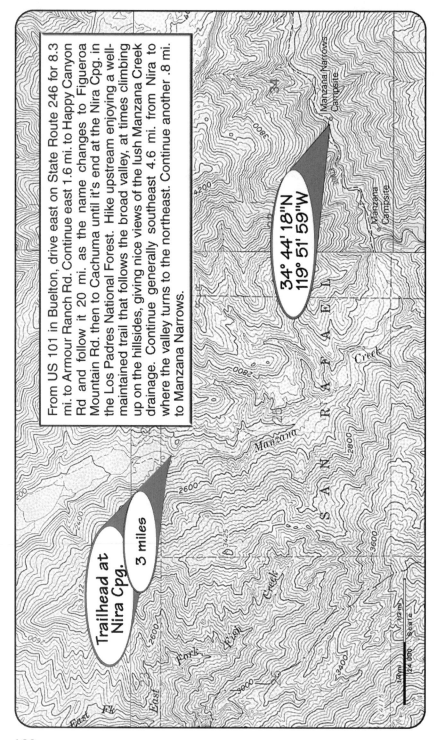

From US 101 in Buelton, drive east on State Route 246 for 8.3 mi. to Armour Ranch Rd. Continue east 1.6 mi. to Happy Canyon Rd and follow it 20 mi. as the name changes to Figueroa Mountain Rd. then to Cachuma until it's end at the Nira Cpg. in the Los Padres National Forest. Hike upstream enjoying a well-maintained trail that follows the broad valley, at times climbing up on the hillsides, giving nice views of the lush Manzana Creek drainage. Continue generally southeast 4.6 mi. from Nira to where the valley turns to the northeast. Continue another .8 mi. to Manzana Narrows.

Trailhead at Nira Cpg.

3 miles

34° 44' 18"N
119° 51' 59"W

Manzana Narrows

A double or triple-spout waterfall depending on how much rain has fallen on San Rafael Mountain. Manzana Narrows is somewhere between a pool and a tub. The western flow of Manzana Creek means great afternoon light. It's not much more than six feet deep. Not a lot of seating available either and that means this is definitely not a place that could absorb lots of visitors. But with the trail camp on a bench above the hole, there's plenty of room to spread out your stuff. The waterfall, about six feet high, is engaging enough and there's plenty of foliage that creates a nice ceiling.

The San Rafael's most famous claim is being the first official wilderness. The Wilderness Act of 1964 converted several places like the San Rafael from federally designated "primitive areas" to federally designated wilderness areas. It took a few years to apply the regulations, but in 1968 the San Rafael earned the distinction.

It's a longish day trip, around seven miles one way. The trail is in good enough shape that you can use trail runners to cover ground quickly. The canyon is relatively straight and wide for the Santa Barbara backcountry. Big views at several points as the trail climbs up on the valley's shoulders before plunging back into the alluvium.

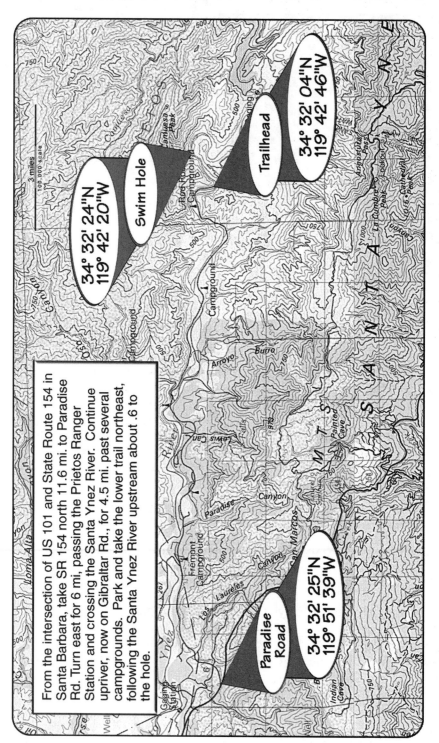

From the intersection of US 101 and State Route 154 in Santa Barbara, take SR 154 north 11.6 mi. to Paradise Rd. Turn east for 6 mi, passing the Prietos Ranger Station and crossing the Santa Ynez River. Continue upriver, now on Gibraltar Rd., for 4.5 mi. past several campgrounds. Park and take the lower trail northeast, following the Santa Ynez River upstream about .6 to the hole.

Swim Hole
34° 32' 24"N
119° 42' 20"W

Trailhead
34° 32' 04"N
119° 42' 46"W

Paradise Road
34° 32' 25"N
119° 51' 39"W

Red Rocks

The Santa Ynez River below Gibralter Dam has several dandy basins. Problem is they're all next to the road and during the summer are overrun by the boom box brigades. Red Rocks is a good hole that's accessible but not too crowded. It's got an irregular shape, making it less attractive than it could be. A nice-sized rock in the middle of the pool stands four feet above surface and serves as a fine diving platform for kids or those who don't value big vertical. There's a modest, crescent shaped sand bar at one end for lounging.

I spent the night at Red Rocks and was startled by a tremendous splash. "Rock fall," my friend said. After a few minutes there was another big splash. We shined our headlamps into the river and determined that under no circumstances could a rock have fallen into the deep water without us first hearing it bounce off some other rocks. It's dark, we're alone and facing an unexplained phenomenon with nothing but a Swiss Army knife to defend ourselves. After an hour of listening for more splashes and potential banjo music, we got to sleep.

Later we determined that it was a beaver whacking his tail on the water because we made *him* nervous. Talk about irony.

From the mission in Santa Barbara drive up Mission Canyon Rd to Foothill Rd. and turn right. At the fire station turn left and continue up Mission Canyon .25 mi. to Tunnel Rd. Follow it one mile to end. Park and walk about .75 mi. toward the Tunnel Trail. After little more than 100 yards on the Tunnel Trail bear left on the Jesuita Trail and follow that upstream to Seven Falls.

Map Source: DeLorme Topo 3.0

Seven Falls
34° 28' 27"N
119° 42' 20"W

Trailhead
34° 27' 53"N
119° 42' 40"W

HOLLY RD
ORANGE GROVE AVE.
MISSION CANYON RD
PASEO
HOLLY RD
PALOMINO RD
PALOMINO RD
PALOMINO RD
TUNNEL RD
MISSION CANYON RD
LAS CANOAS RD
LAS CANOAS RD
LAS CANOAS RD
LAS CANOAS RD
LAS CANOAS RD
MONTROSE PL
MONTROSE PL
DORKING PL
ANDANTE RD
TORROE RD
EXETER PL
RYE RD
DURA RD
192
CHARLOTTE LN
MISSION CANYON RD
MISSION OAKS LN
GLENDESSARY LN
Mission Canyon
Rattlesnake Canyon
LAS CANOAS LN
TIERRA CIELO LN
FOOTHILL LN
MOUNT CALVARY
CIELITO
WOODALE LN
FAIRWOOD LN
Sheffield

0   .5 mi   1 mi   1.5 mi   2 mi
50,000 Scale

186

Seven Falls

An excellent set of tubs. Seven Falls is steep and narrow with tubs just wide enough for a few people yet deep enough that you can't touch bottom. Waterslides connect a couple of the pools and moss makes the trip a little less bumpy on the user's bottom. There's some diving, but funseekers better have good aim because the sweet spot is mighty small. Lounge space surrounding the tubs is very limited and, since the spot is heavily visited, weekends generally find people perched on rocks packed tight as cormorants.

Mission Creek lies roughly parallel to a tunnel built to bring water from Gibralter Reservoir to Santa Barbara. It seemed like a good idea when, in 1922, city engineers projected the dam would remain a source of water for 900 years. These days it's around 70 percent silted up and officials are trying to figure out what to do with it and dozens of other dams across the state that are also silting up, though at a slower rate than Gibralter.

Wet years favor this spot. It drains a relatively small part of Santa Barbara's front country. Southern exposure means the place gets hot in the summer. Privacy is doubtful.

Bonus Feature: Rock climbers might want to bring a rope to sample the routes above the swimming holes. A couple of them are old enough to have piton scars.

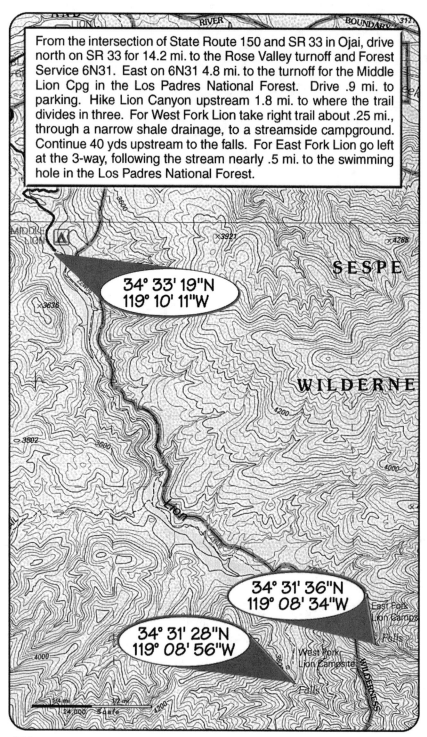

From the intersection of State Route 150 and SR 33 in Ojai, drive north on SR 33 for 14.2 mi. to the Rose Valley turnoff and Forest Service 6N31. East on 6N31 4.8 mi. to the turnoff for the Middle Lion Cpg in the Los Padres National Forest. Drive .9 mi. to parking. Hike Lion Canyon upstream 1.8 mi. to where the trail divides in three. For West Fork Lion take right trail about .25 mi., through a narrow shale drainage, to a streamside campground. Continue 40 yds upstream to the falls. For East Fork Lion go left at the 3-way, following the stream nearly .5 mi. to the swimming hole in the Los Padres National Forest.

34° 33' 19"N
119° 10' 11"W

34° 31' 36"N
119° 08' 34"W

34° 31' 28"N
119° 08' 56"W

West Fork Lion Creek

Sort of an Alice in Wonderland swimming hole in that it's surrounded by polka-dotted rocks. Rounded rocks, perhaps ancient river cobbles, became surrounded by a matrix of softer material which itself metamorphosed into rock. The cobbles were then carried back to the surface locked in the metamorphic rock where we find them millions of years later, once again in a stream. This time water has worn the mixture smooth, thereby making the cobbles appear painstakingly inset in the surrounding rock like paving stones. The swimming area is really just a large tub, nothing too grand, but the surrounding canopy of vegetation gives it a comfortable, cloistered feel. A good place to bring the little dippers.

The trail generally follows Lion Creek. It's fairly flat with only a couple of hills, an excellent trail run for runners of intermediate abilities. Once you get to the creek, the run turns into a low crouch as you bushwhack upstream. Be particularly careful walking in the margins of streams and through water less than one foot deep. Lion Creek is habitat for the endangered Arroyo Toad. It lays eggs in long, gelatinous strands resting in shallow water. The eggs can sometimes look like vegetation as plant life attaches itself to the negatively buoyant strands.

Potrero John
(see Pro Tour)

East Fork Lion Creek

This is probably the better of the two Lion Creek spots. The best part is the water. It's gin clear. Like the west fork, the tubs are deeply shaded, but the understory of vegetation at the east fork is lighter, less tangled. It's a little more vertical with an easy scramble up to the main tub. Perfect for a dunk and a splash during the hot weather of mid summer when the combination of water level and temperature should be optimal.

Check out the deer grass on the way to the swimming hole. The tall reedy bunches of grass turn a short portion of the trail into a tunnel seven feet tall. It looks more like Indonesia than the semiarid Transverse Range. Chumash Indians used it to weave baskets. Also be on the lookout for red-legged frogs, another federally endangered species. They attach egg balls to cattails or willow limbs in ponds similar to the pool below the falls. If you find a ball-shaped, translucent egg mass three inches across, do not disturb it.

Privacy is likely, although the easy access makes this an attractive destination for scout outings. Mountain bikes are permitted, although the trail is short enough and well enough maintained that running shoes are the best footwear.

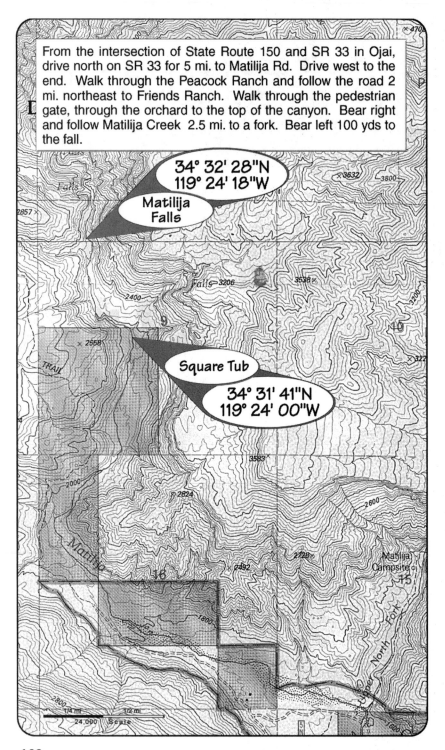

From the intersection of State Route 150 and SR 33 in Ojai, drive north on SR 33 for 5 mi. to Matilija Rd. Drive west to the end. Walk through the Peacock Ranch and follow the road 2 mi. northeast to Friends Ranch. Walk through the pedestrian gate, through the orchard to the top of the canyon. Bear right and follow Matilija Creek 2.5 mi. to a fork. Bear left 100 yds to the fall.

34° 32' 28"N
119° 24' 18"W

Matilija Falls

Square Tub

34° 31' 41"N
119° 24' 00"W

Matilija Creek

If you've only got one day in the Ventura County backcountry, spend it here. A double waterfall creates a tasty pair of holes, deep and alluring. The water is contained in a symmetrical bowl that discharges through a small spout. Usually the stone lip is wide enough that you can recline on it and gaze at the upper fall across a 30-foot pool of cool water.

Although the waterfall is excellent, the trip up the watercourse is even more pleasing. The rock bed is laid down on the same plane as the creek, thus creating some marvelously even slabs that border the pools. Dark shale known as Juncal formation fractures in right angles, creating small bricks that kids love because they're just like building blocks. You'll want to pause at a delightful square tub located near a large boulder on the right bank. The pool is fed by two streams that descend in terraces and enter the pool at right angles to one another. A bower covering the tub gives it a low, geometric outline reminiscent of a Frank Lloyd Wright design.

Once you get up to the main fall, check out another excellent hole just a short trip up the right-hand fork. Northern exposure means summer temperatures are moderated. Walking on the margins of the stream should be avoided where possible because footsteps disturb fish and amphibian eggs laid there.

34° 29' 34"N
118° 58' 29"W

Lower Hole

34° 29' 30"N
118° 56' 56"W

Upper Hole

2500

Park Here

34° 28' 49"N
118° 55' 01"W

Oak Flat

From Fillmore drive north on Goodenough Rd to Squaw Flat Rd. (aka Dough Flat turn off). Follow a winding dirt road 3.2 mi. to a fire station, then continue 1.4 mi. to an unmarked turnout on the left. Park and walk through a metal gate, following the trail 1.8 mi. west to the creek in the Los Padres National Forest. Wade 400 yds downstream to upper hole. For the lower hole, continue about .7 mi. downstream.

Map Source: DeLorme Topo 3.0

Scale

1/4 mi

1/2 mi

1:24,000

Upper Tar Creek

A classic. Tar Creek is a three-tier assembly of smooth sandstone bowls that empty one into another, creating a contour so fine that it's sculptural. The enclosure is superb. Deep, even holes each with a small spout draining into the next pool. The surrounding walls and slabs all seem to perch right over the deepest part of the hole, making for excellent diving. The only negative is limited shade. It gets mighty hot in the summer. Privacy is likely. There's rarely more than one other group here.

This is the first place that California Condors were reintroduced into the wild. Many of the historic nesting sites were here in the Sespe; however the reintroduction encountered difficulties. The wide-ranging birds died from ingesting antifreeze and flying into power lines. They were relocated to a more remote site in the Los Padres. Still, there's a chance you may see one above Tar Creek, especially toward the turn of the century if the population expands as hoped.

Bonus Feature: If you climb, bring shoes. There's excellent, though difficult, bouldering surrounding the holes.

Tar Creek

Lower Tar Creek

For those who want privacy and can pay the price. Located about one-half mile below the aforementioned bowls, Lower Tar Creek is formed where the stream spills over a sheer 90-foot wall. The resultant waterfall empties into a moderately deep, rock-strewn pool filled with jade-colored water. The wall forms an impressive 120-degree enclosure and the loose, muddy matrix of the conglomerate rock makes the crumbled boulders at the bottom look like some ancient Etruscan ruin. Strenuous boulder hopping downstream takes you to a second hole at the bottom of a smaller fall. A long white sandstone wall gives this hole a more even contour. The lines are simply bent, whereas the lines of the hole above are tangled. The lower hole is the nicer of the two.

Best way in is rappel. Bring plenty of runner to anchor on some sycamore trees about 20 yards back from the main falls. Once you rappel in, you're best advised to use ascenders or prusiks to get back out, since the rock is extremely loose. Not a good idea to climb it even on a top rope lest you shower your belay with rockfall.

Best after wet winters. Tar Creek is a small watershed and the water can get dark and stagnant later in the year, but in early summer it's delightful and the long approach keeps the riffraff out.

Why Bother

Punchbowl

Too well known and too little loved. Tremendously beautiful but with litter, graffiti and rowdy crowds. Wildlife is mostly in the form of drinking and the boom box brigades.

Ten-foot hole

Right by the Lion Cpg. Rowdy crowds.

Tangerine Falls

Very popular day trip. Very pretty fall. Not swimmable though.

Mono Debris Dam

Mondo slide off the front of the dam, but man-made structure, so it's out.

San Gabriel & San Bernardino Mtns.

From the intersection of I-210 and SR 39 in Azusa, drive north on SR 39 for 13 mi to Devil's Canyon Dam Road and the Cogswell Reservoir. The road is gated, so the only practical way up is bicycle. It's a 500-foot elevation gain over 7 mi. of paved road. The last mile is leg-breaker steep. Cross the dam to the north and follow a dirt road left until it ends. At the end there's a steep, informal trail that leads down to the reservoir. From there you have a knee-bashing boulder hop .75 mi. north to the pool in the Angeles National Forest. Total distance from the dam is 2.5 mi.

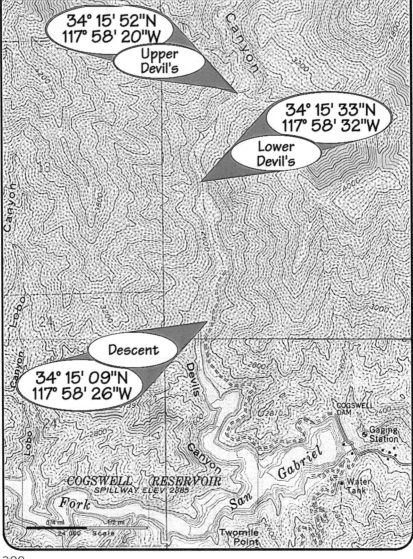

34° 15' 52"N
117° 58' 20"W

Upper
Devil's

34° 15' 33"N
117° 58' 32"W

Lower
Devil's

Descent

34° 15' 09"N
117° 58' 26"W

COGSWELL   DAM

Gaging
Station

Water
Tank

COGSWELL   RESERVOIR
SPILLWAY ELEV 2885

Fork

Twomile
Point

Lower Devils Canyon

Water to your earlobes is the only way to endure summer heat at the mouth of Devils Canyon. Steep walls discourage shade trees and the flat horizon of the reservoir below means light continues to grill the swimming hole well into the afternoon. But if you visit in the spring, there's a sweet, sweet pool. It's eight to ten feet deep with pale green water that's cool as jade. Further proof that nature is merciful: A little alder clings to a ledge, providing the barest umbrella of shade right over the deep end of the pool.

An extremely narrow constriction in the canyon helped produce this feature. The pool is fed by a small cascade that runs between steep walls less than 40 feet apart at the top. Gorgeous views of the reservoir and surrounding mountains through the canyon's rifle-sight notch. If you continue up-canyon, there are at least one dozen tubs, a few pools and all the solitude you need. The best spot is a small tub where the water makes a tight 180-degree turn, running over your shoulders, across your belly and through your toes before rushing back up your leg and exiting downstream. The adjoining slabs are polished smooth and tilted at a perfect angle for an afternoon nap.

There are only three maintained trails in the San Gabriel Wilderness, and this isn't one of them. Plan to get wet during the approach. Privacy is just about guaranteed in the upper tubs.

Beyond
Nowhere

34° 17' 45"N
117° 44' 28"W

Bridge to
Nowhere

34° 16' 59"N
117° 44' 44"W

From the intersection of I-210 and State Route 39 in Azusa, drive north on SR 39 11.8 mi to the East Fork Rd. Drive east for 5.8 mi. to the ranger station. Fill out a wilderness permit and hike north for 4.6 mi. to "The Bridge to Nowhere," a remnant from an abandoned highway project. Continue past the bridge, through The Narrows to a point just above a 450-foot-high escarpment running east to west just below the Iron Fork of the San Gabriel River.

Beyond Nowhere

A swimming hole made for two. Any more would be a crowd, any fewer a shame. A splendidly smooth boulder sits smack in the middle of the stream with an alder bough hanging over it. On the right side, water-worn ledges sweep up to a wall with jumping ledges at 7, 10, 12 and 20 feet. Get a good launch, 'cause there's a slight ledge underneath. Water quality is remarkable. The East Fork of the San Gabriel happens to be the definition of Coke-bottle green. Early in the season much of the water will be snow runoff from Mt. Baldy, which sits on the eastern boundary of Sheep Mountain Wilderness.

The Narrows is the deepest gorge in Southern California. The depth of the canyon, coupled with the abandoned bridge downstream, attracted the attention of bungee jumpers like Ron Jones who bought the bridge from its private owner. If you visit during a weekend, chances are you'll see Jones flinging paying customers over the side.

You'll find a couple of pools right below the bridge that can be reached by crossing the bridge, turning left and scrambling down. There are several stream crossings, so plan to get wet on the way up. Plan on company, too. During summer there may be as many as 100 people on the lower part of the trail, although only a fraction make it as far as the bridge and fewer still could be expected to make it to The Narrows.

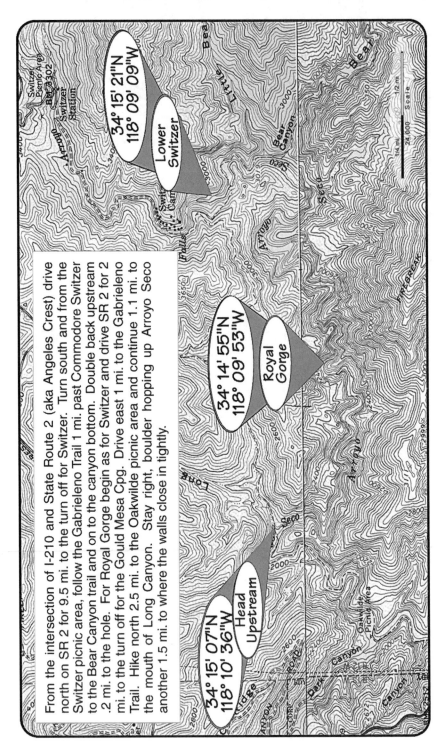

From the intersection of I-210 and State Route 2 (aka Angeles Crest) drive north on SR 2 for 9.5 mi. to the turn off for Switzer. Turn south and from the Switzer picnic area, follow the Gabrieleno Trail 1 mi. past Commodore Switzer to the Bear Canyon trail and on to the canyon bottom. Double back upstream .2 mi. to the hole. For Royal Gorge begin as for Switzer and drive SR 2 for 2 mi. to the turn off for the Gould Mesa Cpg. Drive east 1 mi. to the Gabrieleno Trail. Hike north 2.5 mi. to the Oakwilde picnic area and continue 1.1 mi. to the mouth of Long Canyon. Stay right, boulder hopping up Arroyo Seco another 1.5 mi. to where the walls close in tightly.

34° 15' 21"N
118° 09' 09"W

Lower Switzer

34° 14' 55"N
118° 09' 53"W

Royal Gorge

34° 15' 07"N
118° 10' 36"W

Head Upstream

Lower Switzer Falls

Perfect dimensions for a low-altitude cannonball. On its way down from Switzer Campground, water pauses in a dandy tub about twenty feet wide and seven feet deep. There are two falls and it's the upper one that's the nicer. A four-foot-high, solid rock wall impounds the stream on the downhill side. It also creates a nice chute of water that empties into the lower pool which is just barely deep enough for splashing around. The upper tub, with its sloping side walls that offer the perfect launch, is worthy of an excellent rating, but human impact reduces it to simply good. The place is Bedlam on the weekends. Dozens of people will make the trip down from Switzer Falls proper. There are bottles, wrappers, some graffiti and a type of litter unique to swimming holes—cotton socks. As it turns out, socks are a pretty reliable index to how heavily visited a swimming hole is. Lower Switzer posted a staggering ten socks on the spring weekend in which it was surveyed. If you value privacy, go elsewhere.

Be aware that the right-hand traverse above the first pool is potentially dangerous. The rock is somewhat loose. The most tempting steps are on tree roots, but this is a bad idea. Stepping on and around tree roots causes damage to the root, erosion and eventually death of the tree. Be responsible and avoid injuring the plants that create a moist, shaded space within the otherwise sun-bleached landscape of the Angeles.

Royal Gorge

Royal Gorge

Perhaps not royal, but certainly noble. The gorge is actually a section of Arroyo Seco where the watercourse zigzags among steep walls rising more than 500 feet above the streambed. This excellent hole is located near the top of the gorge. A 50-foot-high rock forms the left-hand wall of the hole. It sweeps down to the stream bed where the water slides along a 45-degree slope before free falling into a tank that's about ten feet deep in the middle. The surface area measures 50 feet by 30 feet and the contours are generally even. All in all, an outstanding place to spend an early summer day.

But you won't be able to spend much of the day there unless you get an early start. Royal Gorge is tough to get to and can take a fit hiker more than three hours in. Bring a walking stick and plan on getting your feet wet. You'll be high stepping and winding back and forth through the gorge's many horseshoe turns. Alternately you can approach Royal Gorge by heading downstream from Switzer; however, getting into the hole itself requires a rope. It may seem otherwise, like you could slide right down the chute into the hole. Don't. If you look closely there's a ledge under the falls and if you hit it, chances are excellent that your tailbone will become lodged in your kidneys. A scramble around the south wall is equally dicey since the rock is quite fractured.

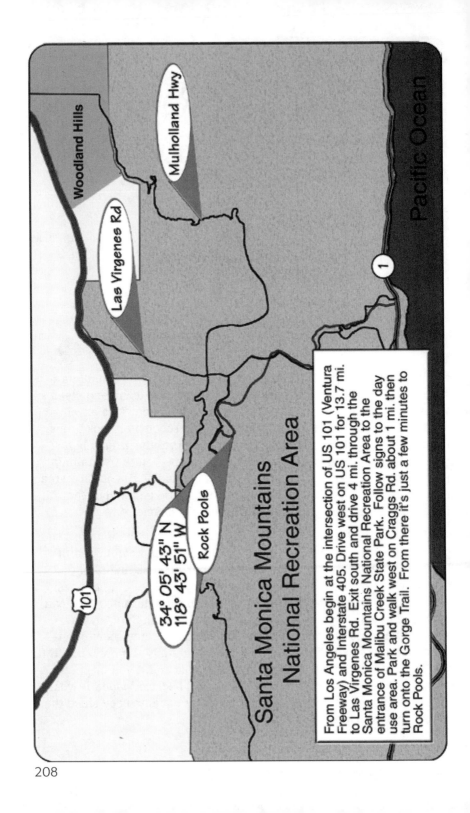

Woodland Hills

Las Virgenes Rd

Mulholland Hwy

Pacific Ocean

101

1

34° 05' 43" N
118° 43' 51" W

Rock Pools

Santa Monica Mountains
National Recreation Area

From Los Angeles begin at the intersection of US 101 (Ventura
Freeway) and Interstate 405. Drive west on US 101 for 13.7 mi.
to Las Virgenes Rd. Exit south and drive 4 mi. through the
Santa Monica Mountains National Recreation Area to the
entrance of Malibu Creek State Park. Follow signs to the day
use area. Park and walk west on Craggs Rd. about 1 mi. then
turn onto the Gorge Trail. From there it's just a few minutes to
Rock Pools.

Rock Pools

Easy to get to and hard to forget. Malibu Creek spreads out just below a volcanic canyon into a big, fine piece of water more than 60 feet wide. The walls are filled with pockets typical of volcanic rock, the same features that make Malibu Creek State Park among the best rock climbing spots on the Southern California coast. Several truck-sized boulders on the upstream side provide modest launch platforms. Diving is officially prohibited in state parks and it's easy to understand why – many drunken yahoos going head-first into the water. They look like a how-to video for head trauma. Use some sense, please.

If you're a fan of old movies, the backdrop may look somewhat familiar. Before it was a park, Paramount Studios owned the ranch and used it as a filming location. Rock Pools served as an outdoor set for the *Swiss Family Robinson*, *South Pacific* and *Tarzan* movies. It's assumed that any crocodiles Tarzan tussled with were removed after filming.

As nice as this place may be, prepare to share. Malibu Creek is a multi-cultural extravaganza on weekends. At less than one hour from the center of Los Angeles, it's not unusual to find 40 or more people here, making it a boisterous place — boom boxes and all. Nevertheless it's scrupulously maintained. You'll find no visible graffiti and the litter (of which there is plenty) is quickly picked up by park personnel.

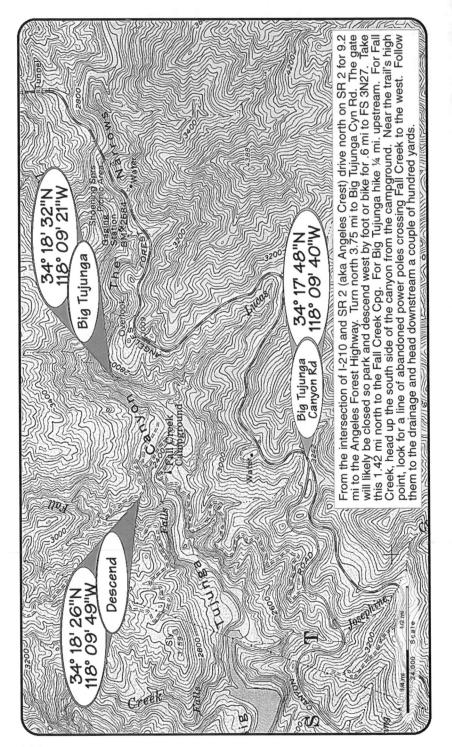

From the intersection of I-210 and SR 2 (aka Angeles Crest) drive north on SR 2 for 9.2 mi to the Angeles Forest Highway. Turn north 3.75 mi to Big Tujunga Cyn Rd. The gate will likely be closed so park and descend west by foot or bike for .6 mi to FS 3N27. Take this 1.42 mi north to the Fall Creek Cpg. For Big Tujunga hike ¼ mi. upstream. For Fall Creek, head up the south side of the canyon from the campground. Near the trail's high point, look for a line of abandoned power poles crossing Fall Creek to the west. Follow them to the drainage and head downstream a couple of hundred yards.

34° 18' 32"N
118° 09' 21"W

Big Tujunga

34° 17' 48"N
118° 09' 40"W

Big Tujunga
Canyon Rd

34° 18' 26"N
118° 09' 49"W

Descend

Big Tujunga

People. Big Tujunga Creek suffers from them. The deep canyon between Colby Ranch and the Angeles Forest Highway could easily be the most charming watercourse in the Angeles, but for the quantity of beer cans, the proliferation of litter and worst of all, graffiti. One spot *is* worth visiting. Below the bridge, the creek bounces along between brittle canyon walls and through a small fall opposite a 200-foot-high, northwest facing wall. At the bottom of the fall is a basin that's around six feet deep and fringed with alder, including a clump of young trees precariously perched in the middle of the creek directly above the fall. The alders, combined with the steep canyon walls, prevent direct sunlight from penetrating until late afternoon when the rays shine on a smooth granite slab that's the dimension of a single bed.

It was while crouching through the alders that, unknown to me, a branch got lodged between my pack and torso. When I stood up straight, I felt something hit me in the back of the legs. This, following a week during which I'd seen more than seven rattlesnakes. Instantly, I was in full flight, high stepping and hyperventilating for 50 yards before I realized I was swatting myself in the butt with a tree branch. Thankfully, there were no witnesses.

Apart from such incidents the approach is not at all difficult, but longish. Perfect for the novice hiker who wants a challenge.

Long Point

part of *Southeastern Swimming Holes*, a colleciton of destinations from the Virginias through the Carolinas, Georgia and north Florida.

Fall Creek

Rare is the swimming hole that needs more use. Fall Creek is one. Located well above Big Tujunga, this creek falls 300 feet to the canyon bottom, pausing along the way in a few difficult-to-reach tubs that contain an awful lot of plant goo. A bit of splashing about ought to stir the water up enough to flush the moss and so forth into the lower and middle portions of the fall which aren't especially attractive as a swimming hole. The upper tub is a different story altogether. A 40-foot, free-falling steam of water leaps over a ledge and tumbles into a deep, dark cavity in the rock. The tub is ten feet wide and seven-feet deep. Water drains over the lip, down a 20-foot granite slab and into another pool. The flow then turns left along a narrow shelf, around a mature willow and over a second, larger fall into a shallow pool 70 feet below.

Privacy is guaranteed. Consequently, getting there is a blister. In addition to rope skills, you need the patience to endure some fifth-class bushwhacking down a nearly nonexistent trail to the creek. Kind of like walking through an automatic car wash with the water turned off. From there it's a short trip along the brush-choked stream to the lip. To the right of the falls are some trees you can rapp off of. Bring a couple of double runners at least 80 feet of rope, more if you want to rappel on a double rope and climb back out on top rope. (Hint: If you don't understand the previous sentence, don't go.)

From Lake Arrowhead in the San Bernardino National Forest, follow State Route 173 along the south shore to Hook Creek Rd. Take Hook Creek until the pavement ends and continue on forest service road 3N34 to a fork. Bear left about .5 mi. to Splinter's Cabin. (Note: the road appears ill advised for passenger cars, yet many make the trip.) Take the Pacific Crest Trail north for a little less than 2 mi. and you'll see Gilligan's Island back over your shoulder. The descent is about .25 mi. farther north at 34° 17' 57"N and 117° 07' 28"W. For Center Cut continue north on the PCT past the OHV road to Bacon Flats and then about 1 mi. farther. Descent trails are sketchy. You might want to descend at the first good trail you find, then boulder hop downstream.

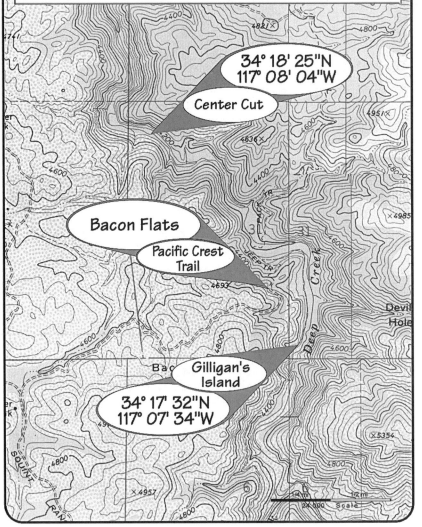

The Cliffs

A place to build your courage. The jumps are evenly spaced from five feet high to about thirty-five feet so you can work your way up. It's 25 minutes upstream from the road, past several other holes that, while objectively good, are ruined by broken beer bottles, etc. After some easy scrambling over granite blocks and around trees you'll get to the spot recognizable by the diving cliff on the left-hand side and a black cable fixed there to help jumpers back to the diving ledges. The water is ten to twelve feet deep, but you can't see the bottom since visibility in Deep Creek is about seven feet. Submerged rocks are not always visible. Best ask the locals where the sweet spot is.

And you shouldn't have trouble finding locals for advice. Expect as many as one dozen people here on a hot weekend. The prime sunning ledges are on the right, directly across from the diving rock and a great vantage point. About ten people will fit here and another dozen can be accommodated on a second, lower ledge that's also on the right just downstream from the diving rock. It's all fairly close together, so you have to be neighborly.

If it's just too crowded you may want to boulder hop ten minutes upstream to a quiet pool that's around seven feet deep with an even bottom. By far the most appealing feature is the smooth slab upstream from the pool where the water rolls over the rock in a broad sheet before slipping over the lip and into the pool. If The Cliffs are the recreation room of the house, this would be the study.

Aztec Falls

Aztec Falls

Probably the best diving spot in Southern California. If Aztec Falls were a ski area, it would be Squaw Valley. Steep and deep. The main rock is on the left, directly adjoining the falls. Locals say it goes up to 57 feet. The landing will be 15 feet deep or more. Intermediate ledges offer more modest jumps—30 feet or so! The fall itself is less imposing, but you can tell by the depth of the canyon that this river gets angry. Everything's here: jumps, slabs to sun on, sand bars to nap on.

Problem is you aren't likely to get much sleep. There may be as many as one dozen people having fun on a summer weekend. Litter is not an apparent problem. Volunteer groups like the Fisheries Volunteer Resource Corps keep this and other parts of the river picked up. The volunteers operate two-person patrols throughout the Deep Creek drainage, packing out everything from potato chip bags to automobile tires. They also help with trail maintenance and graffiti removal. You'll recognize them by the volunteer patch they wear on the standard forest service uniform.

Try and make sure they don't have to carry you out. It is easy to get seriously hurt jumping 50 feet or more. Check with locals for submerged obstacles before you jump. *You're responsible for your own safety.*

San Bernardino & San Gabriel Mountains

Peace

Peace

Deep Creek drains the area between Lake Arrowhead and Big Bear. Geographically speaking it's the East Fork of the Mojave River. Say Mojave and you think desert, but this is one beautiful channel of water. Most of the holes are partially visible from the trail, which diminishes privacy, but makes for an incredibly scenic approach. Parts of the canyon are sheer, comprised of a 50-foot-tall line of columns and buttresses all capped by square boulders four to five feet wide. It looks like a ruined colonnade or a row of drunken soldiers with their hats on crooked. It's the sort of place that, on a spring day, you'd expect to find Huck and Tom skipping school.

Peace is not the best diving spot, but it is a tremendously beautiful pool about eight-feet deep and interspersed with small, round boulders. A couple of red firs adjoin the hole and the upstream bank is dominated by a mature ponderosa. If you're visiting during the late spring you should be on the lookout for prickly poppies. It looks like a thistle, but with a bloom so big and white, it's arguably the prettiest wildflower in the state. They grow all over Deep Creek, especially around Devil's Hole and the northern part of forest service road 3N34 near Bacon Flats. The area burned in 1995 and the prickly poppy favors disturbed soil. Look for them also on the side of roadbeds or well drained southern slopes as high as 8,000 feet..

From the town of Crest Park take State Route 173 north for 3.1 mi. through Lake Arrowhead to Hook Creek Rd. Travel east 3 mi. on Hook Creek, then bear left a short distance on Squint Ranch Rd. to a right hand descent that leads .45 mi. to Splinter's Cabin and access to the Pacific Crest Trail. Hike north (downstream) on the PCT .2 mi. to the spur trail for Peace and .4 mi. to the descent for Aztec.

For the Cliffs, rather than go to the PCT access, continue on Hook Creek and drive as far as you dare towards Deep Creek. Where the road crosses the creek take an unmaintained trail on the right-hand bank that leads over steep, loose dirt slopes about 25 minutes upstream to the hole. Boots are recommended.

34° 16' 47"N
117° 07' 41"W

Aztec Falls

34° 16' 38"N
117° 07' 39"W

Peace

Left on 3N34
to PCT access

Splinter's
Cabin

34° 15' 55"N
117° 07' 38"W

The Cliffs

Center Cut

It just keeps coming. One eye-popping place after another. Center Cut is metamorphic rock cooked to perfection in a prehistoric oven, carved by the river and dressed with smooth sand ladled onto the sides like a well-executed bernaise sauce. Water is ten to twelve feet deep with a wedge of rock tipped out and over the tenderloin of the hole, begging you, just begging you, to step off into the water. The top of the hole is occupied by a low, rounded boulder worn smooth by the water and warmed by the southern sun. Alders fringe it, but provide little practical shade. However, at the foot of the pool you'll find a sand bar big enough to park a cattle truck on.

And you night notice some cloven hoof tracks there. Evidently some hunters have introduced Russian boars to the area for their entertainment. Resource managers are appalled. Pigs are rooting animals and, as such, highly destructive, especially in a dry environment that will regenerate slowly. A recent fire scorched the hillsides, but left the river canyon largely untouched. The area was closed for some time to allow regrowth, but the jeep trail across the Pacific Crest Trail was recently reopened. You may find yourself sharing about one mile of trail with motorbikes. Louder vehicles may be audible from the swimming hole.

Gilligan's Island

Gilligan's Island

Deep Creek is a hall of champions. It's easily the best swimming river in the state of California. Gilligan's Island clinches it.

A giant, globular pyramid of rock dominates the center of the river with steep canyon walls rising up on each side. Not a lot of seating and the shade is somewhat limited, but lots of nice sedges and grasses give it a well dressed look. The scramble up the diving rock is challenging. Rock climbing skills are a plus, if not a necessity. Depth is around 12 feet.

Visitors are mostly local, mostly young. Matthew Schwab is one of them. Schwab and his friends regularly jump 40 feet from the top of the pyramid. He says the most frightening aspect of Gilligan's Island isn't the height. No, it's the swimming rattlesnakes. Schwab said he routinely finds them sunning on rocks or swimming in the water as if for recreation. Herpetologists are not convinced that a behavioral adaptation is occurring along Deep Creek. Nevertheless be careful you don't resurface under one and end up with a pit viper necklace.

Gilligan's Island is plainly visible from the PCT, but only to those headed south. Since most people hike the trail south to north, they whiz right by it. Also, the spur trail down to the river isn't apparent and once at streamside you have to bushwhack and boulderhop upstream.

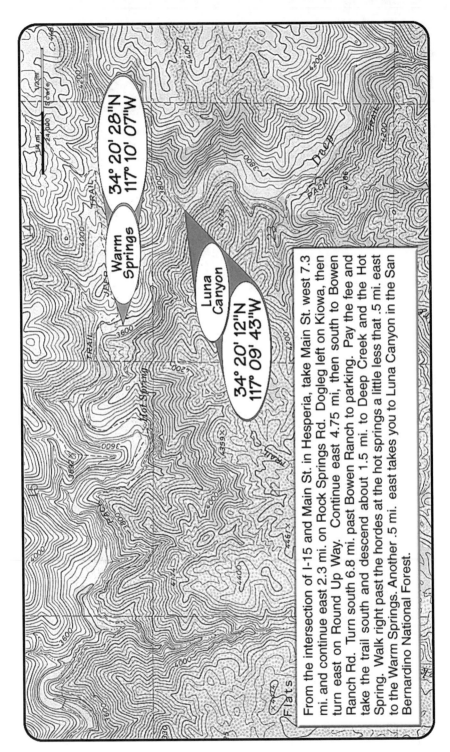

Warm Springs

34° 20' 28"N
117° 10' 07"W

Luna Canyon

34° 20' 12"N
117° 09' 43"W

From the intersection of I-15 and Main St. in Hesperia, take Main St. west 7.3 mi. and continue east 2.3 mi. on Rock Springs Rd. Dogleg left on Kiowa, then turn east on Round Up Way. Continue east 4.75 mi, then south to Bowen Ranch Rd. Turn south 6.8 mi. past Bowen Ranch to parking. Pay the fee and take the trail south and descend about 1.5 mi. to Deep Creek and the Hot Spring. Walk right past the hordes at the hot springs a little less that .5 mi. east to the Warm Springs. Another .5 mi. east takes you to Luna Canyon in the San Bernardino National Forest.

Luna Canyon

Lackadaisical trout and lack of footprints. A medium-sized pool is ringed entirely by granite blocks that stairstep down to a patch of water almost the exact dimensions of what you'd expect to find in a backyard The pool is deepest to the left where the water passes between the pincers of surrounding boulders. A low, broad platform is directly across from the small cascade and a decent sand beach has a sycamore that gives enough shade for a small group.

About 40 yards downstream is a basin with a beach big enough and flat enough for a volleyball game. Must be 50 feet long and 30 feet wide. Better bring two full teams because you're not going to find any pickup players here. Visitation is extremely light. I didn't see one pair of footprints. The basin is 70 feet on the major axis and has a considerable amount of boulder clutter. The depth is little more than six feet, but the privacy is profound. Just about guaranteed.

It's a long damned walk if you approach from Lake Arrowhead, more like a trail run. If you're super fit, this is an awesome trip. Be prepared for a hot return. Although the trail parallels the river, it's usually 100 vertical feet above the water, often higher. You should bring a couple of quarts of water per person to make the return without the time consuming need to descend and filter.

Lower Calf Creek

part of *Southwestern Swimming Holes*, a survey of 200 creeks and canyons from the high plateaus of Utah to the Mexican border.

Warm Springs

Yeah, everybody loves a hot spring and there's a well-known one on Deep Creek. Way too crowded and not much of a swimming hole anyway. Disappointment turned to delight upstream at Warm Spring which receives a fraction of the visitors. The spring comes from the steep rock wall on the north side of the creek and the warm water is contained in a couple of rock tubs. The creek is around 20 feet wide and a good eight-feet deep just below the tubs. That works out to a Finnish style thermal treatment where you can soak in the warm bath water then plunge into the cool river and feel the tingle as your pores snap shut.

Calling this a "warm spring" is somewhat dismissive. Although not as hot its downstream cousin, as it's still a delightful temperature. A couple of tubs have been fashioned from stone and mortar constructed around a declivity in the hillside. This violates the rule against including any man-made structure in the book, but a great man once said that "foolish consistency is the hobgoblin of a simple mind."

You can approach either from the ranch above or up the Pacific Crest Trail from the west. There are a couple of beautiful swimming holes a little over a mile below the hot springs; however, they were roached with broken glass and trash.

Why Bother

Sturtevant Falls
Fewer people at Disneyland.

Cooper Canyon
Pretty falls. Shallow pool.

San Antonio Falls
Small watershed, puddle at the bottom.

Trail Canyon
Sign says no swimming. People get drinking water from the stream.

Switzer Falls
Sand and gravel-filled basin less than four feet deep.

Fish Fork
Main fall is a sheer 20-footer that unfortunately empties into a shallow pool.

Santa Ana & Laguna Mountains

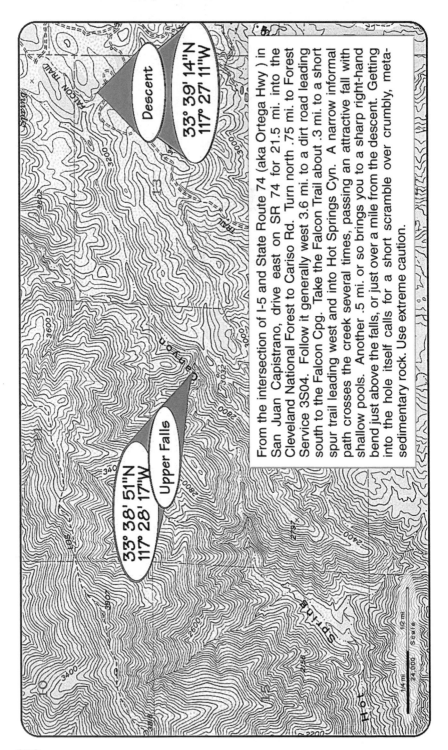

Descent

33° 39' 14"N
117° 27' 11"W

Upper Falls

33° 38' 51"N
117° 28' 17"W

From the intersection of I-5 and State Route 74 (aka Ortega Hwy) in San Juan Capistrano, drive east on SR 74 for 21.5 mi. into the Cleveland National Forest to Cariso Rd. Turn north .75 mi. to Forest Service 3S04. Follow it generally west 3.6 mi. to a dirt road leading south to the Falcon Cpg. Take the Falcon Trail about .3 mi. to a short spur trail leading west and into Hot Springs Cyn. A narrow informal path crosses the creek several times, passing an attractive fall with shallow pools. Another .5 mi. or so brings you to a sharp right-hand bend just above the falls, or just over a mile from the descent. Getting into the hole itself calls for a short scramble over crumbly, meta-sedimentary rock. Use extreme caution.

Hot Springs Canyon

I wept. Upper Hot Springs is a cylinder bored straight into the rock. The left wall rises 50 feet and the right wall is 30 feet. Between them is a hole ten feet deep—maybe more early in the season. Ferns, mosses and alders contrast sharply with the horned lizards and hard, dry chaparral above. The picture is completed by a two-person sunning rock where the light shines smooth as honey. The fall is a 25-foot chute of polished granite. Jumping ledges present an irresistible temptation. They stair step up the left-hand wall in three-foot increments to a height of 15 feet. Be aware that the higher ledges lean out over a submerged shelf. Check it out before you jump.

Getting to Hot Springs Canyon requires some minor bushwhacking, route-finding skills and scrambling. The last couple of hundred yards to the hole itself is steep and brittle. The rock is extremely loose and the fall would be a long one. Nevertheless, visitorship is fairly high. Privacy is unlikely on a weekend and the approach has more poison oak than I've seen anywhere. Seriously, even if you tried to cultivate the plant commercially, I don't think you could produce a more abundant crop.

From I-15 in Lake Elsinore, take Clinton Keith Rd south as it changes names to Tenaja Rd for a total of 11.2 mi. Turn north on the Tenaja Truck Rd for .5 mi. to the Tenaja Guard Station and continue 4.2 mi. to the San Mateo Canyon Wilderness. Park in a clearing on the west side of the road. From there descend by foot into San Mateo Cyn and follow the old road across the creek. This will probably be a wet ford. It's about .7 mi. up the abandoned road to the top falls.

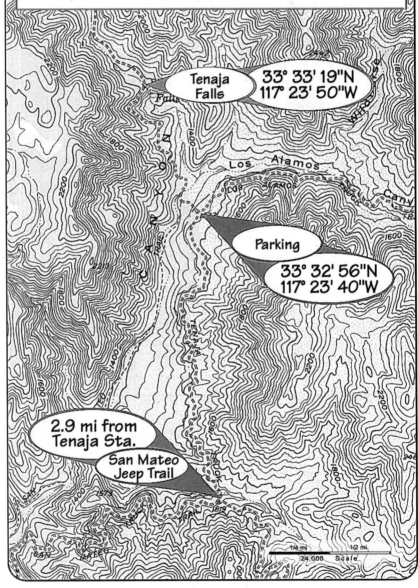

Tenaja Falls
33° 33' 19"N
117° 23' 50"W

Parking
33° 32' 56"N
117° 23' 40"W

2.9 mi from Tenaja Sta.
San Mateo Jeep Trail

Tenaja Falls

Five tiers are spread out along a vertical drop of 140 feet into the floor of Tenaya Creek. The most popular is the top one, a rough oval about 20 feet long on its main axis and around ten feet deep. Water enters through a wedge-shaped gap in the wall above and tumbles 20 feet in two chutes to the main tank. The hole then spills over a would-be slide running 40 feet on a *steep* incline. Problem is the water below the slide is really only a basin which, along with the third pool below it, turns stagnant early in the season. By late May the plant goo index is off the charts.

Excellent views of the falls as you approach from the old Tenaja Road below. Used to be the road went all the way up to the fall. The designation of the San Mateo Canyon Wilderness closed the road in 1984. One of the state's newest designated wilderness areas, it occupies a triangle of peace and quiet between the guns of Camp Pendleton, the roar of water craft on Lake Elsinore, and the urban din of southern Orange County.

Getting to the lower pools is sketchy; I used a rope and a visiting boy scout troop that was picking up garbage was happy to use my line to get up the slab between the top hole and the second pool. The scouts regularly remove litter. Still there's plenty left behind. Despite the closed road, high visitorship means beer, boom boxes and litter.

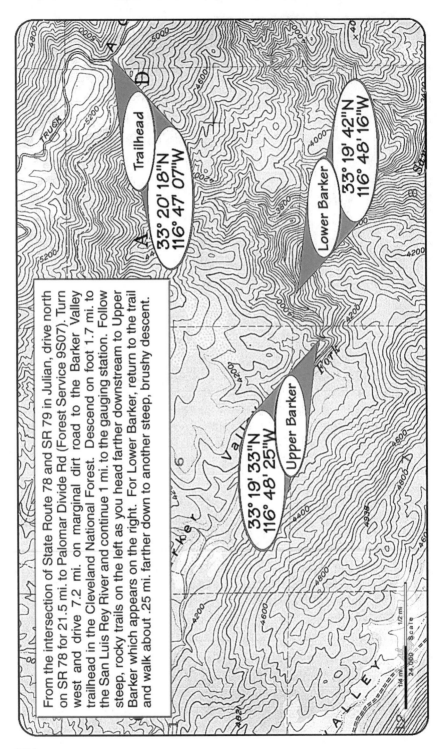

From the intersection of State Route 78 and SR 79 in Julian, drive north on SR 78 for 21.5 mi. to Palomar Divide Rd (Forest Service 9S07). Turn west and drive 7.2 mi. on marginal dirt road to the Barker Valley trailhead in the Cleveland National Forest. Descend on foot 1.7 mi. to the San Luis Rey River and continue 1 mi. to the gauging station. Follow steep, rocky trails on the left as you head farther downstream to Upper Barker which appears on the right. For Lower Barker, return to the trail and walk about .25 mi. farther down to another steep, brushy descent.

Trailhead
33° 20' 18"N
116° 47' 07"W

Lower Barker
33° 19' 42"N
116° 48' 16"W

Upper Barker
33° 19' 33"N
116° 48' 25"W

Upper Barker Valley

Bring sun block. Upper Barker Fall is bare granite with nary a twig of vegetation. The fall is 30 feet high, a cascade that should have enough hydrologic force to bore out a big hole. A big, *deep* hole. But the West Fork of the San Luis Rey River drains only 12 square miles on the leeward side of Palomar Mountain where annual precipitation is around 20 inches—half the total on the windward slope. Consequently, the hole is rarely more than eight feet deep. Hardly ideal for diving, but dyno fine for escaping the heat, of which there is much. The southeast facing canyon heats up early and by midday the sun strikes like a hammer and you're sitting on the anvil.

Paradoxically it can get downright cold in the early morning. As air on Palomar Mountain's upper slopes cools, it becomes heavier than the warm air below, so it slides downhill like water. Cross just about any drainage in the evening and you'll likely notice the air is ten degrees cooler, or more. The contrast in Barker Valley is extreme. If you camp there it's not unheard of to find frost along the stream bed even in July!

Moderate weekend use. Peak weekends can draw a half dozen cars to the trailhead. Most hikers won't make it down to the first falls and fewer still will make the steep trip over a loose trail to the lower fall. The surrounding rock is steep with a few slabs to relax on.

Cedar Creek Falls

Lower Barker Valley

Certainly the better dressed of the Barker Valley Falls. The lower fall has a nice basin about 40 feet wide that's skirted by mature willow, sycamore and at least one ancient oak that provides deep, reliable shade. This is a steep bowl with vertical rock on either side of a 40-foot fall. The enclosure isn't as steep or sculpted as Upper Barker, although the descending spur trail is steep and rock strewn. Brushy to boot. The bottom is broken and uneven. It's usually seven feet deep around the fall. Water quality is fair with visibility being about six feet. Whatever the shortcomings, Lower Barker is a very private place. Private but not quiet. To be heard you'll have to raise your voice above the sound of rushing water.

Another sound to prepare yourself for would be the whir of rattlesnakes. Spring is the most active swimming season on the San Luis Rey River. It's also prime time for buzz worms. Here are a few bits of folk wisdom that may help you avoid snakes, or at least stop worrying about them. A striking snake can reach no more than half the length of its body. In many cases the animal doesn't inject any venom. The most effective item in any snakebite kit is a car key. Meaning, skip the razor blades and suction devices. Just get to a hospital.

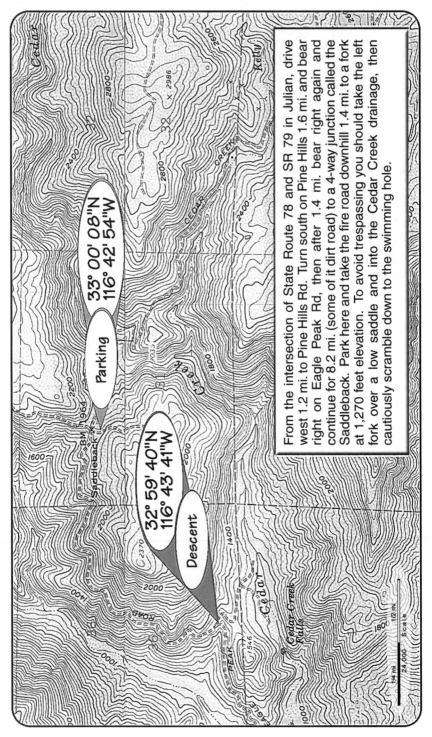

From the intersection of State Route 78 and SR 79 in Julian, drive west 1.2 mi. to Pine Hills Rd. Turn south on Pine Hills 1.6 mi. and bear right on Eagle Peak Rd, then after 1.4 mi. bear right again and continue for 8.2 mi. (some of it dirt road) to a 4-way junction called the Saddleback. Park here and take the fire road downhill 1.4 mi. to a fork at 1,270 feet elevation. To avoid trespassing you should take the left fork over a low saddle and into the Cedar Creek drainage, then cautiously scramble down to the swimming hole.

Parking

33° 00' 08"N
116° 42' 54"W

Descent

32° 59' 40"N
116° 43' 41"W

Cedar Creek Falls

A place of startling beauty and, like many beautiful things, it suffers from over exposure and misuse. It's scuba deep and wide enough for water ballet. The fall itself is a strapping, single channel of water that spills 90 feet into a bowl with steep shoulders. Downstream the sides flare out and flatten into dry space for lounging directly opposite the fall's face. Cottonwoods keep the sun off and there's a sycamore shaded grotto on the right-hand side that you can swim to for sanctuary if the boom box brigades show up.

Cedar Creek Falls has been a favorite day trip for generations of San Diegans. Before the Helix Water District built El Capitan reservoir in the '30s, people used to be able to drive to the falls. Now the trip requires a steep hike down a gated road paralleling the Upper San Diego River. Most people hike to the end of the road where the water district has posted a No Trespassing sign, then walk about one-quarter mile upstream to the swimming hole.

On a peak weekend you might expect to find as many as a couple of dozen people. Inevitably, they leave litter. If you see people littering, return the trash to them and politely say, "Excuse me, I think you dropped this." Confronted with the empty potato chip bag or beer can, most people mumble and act embarrassed.

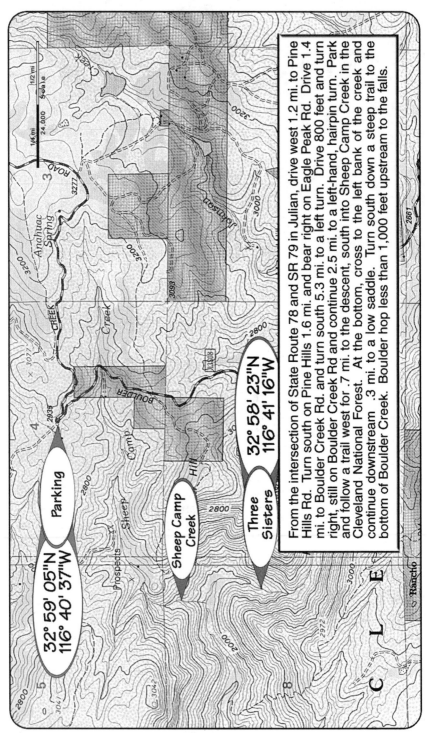

From the intersection of State Route 78 and SR 79 in Julian, drive west 1.2 mi. to Pine Hills Rd. Turn south on Pine Hills 1.6 mi. and bear right on Eagle Peak Rd. Drive 1.4 mi. to Boulder Creek Rd. and turn south 5.3 mi. to a left turn. Drive 800 feet and turn right, still on Boulder Creek Rd and continue 2.5 mi. to a left-hand, hairpin turn. Park and follow a trail west for .7 mi. to the descent, south into Sheep Camp Creek in the Cleveland National Forest. At the bottom, cross to the left bank of the creek and continue downstream .3 mi. to a low saddle. Turn south down a steep trail to the bottom of Boulder Creek. Boulder hop less than 1,000 feet upstream to the falls.

Parking
32° 59' 05"N
116° 40' 37"W

Sheep Camp Creek

Three Sisters
32° 58' 23"N
116° 41' 16"W

Three Sisters

Julian locals *love* this place. As the name implies, there are three falls, each one a big, smooth granite bowl. They are, in every sense, swimming holes that stand out. At one point on the approach, after crossing a low saddle, you suddenly get a full frontal view of the falls filling the head of a steep canyon. The three falls are between 40 and 50 feet tall. The middle hole is around 60 feet wide, 10 feet deep with ample granite slabs to relax on. The uppermost is the trophy hole—the "hog hole." To reach it, scramble left around the second falls and you'll be able to drop into the upper bowl. It's a big ol' tank of water with a 25-foot rock face on the right side which has launched generations of splash rangers. Summer afternoons are long. You can get some relief from the sun in the cottonwoods below the lowest bowl, but there are few comfortable rocks among the trees as compared with the comfortable though sun-stunned slabs surrounding the upper bowls.

Turbidity is about the only bad thing there is to say about this hole. When I visited in mid April, Boulder Creek had poor visibility. It may have been the result of a recent forest fire or it may be due to the fact that it carries discharge from Cuyamaca Reservoir. Late summer and early fall may be bad times to visit as the flow from the Cuyamaca Reservoir is generally reduced. And watch for poison oak. It flourishes along the Boulder Creek.

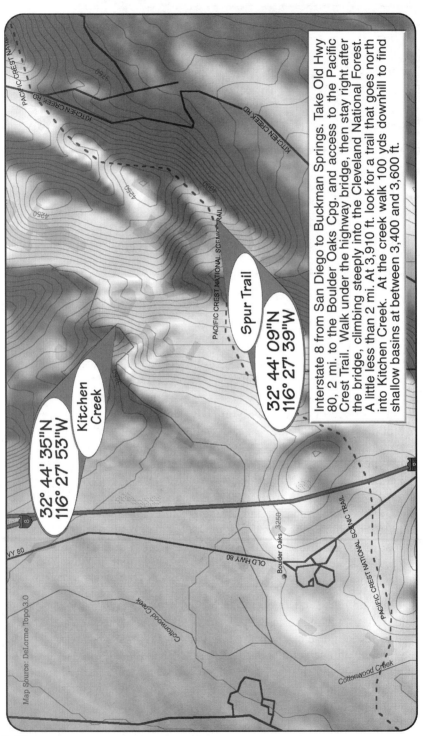

Interstate 8 from San Diego to Buckman Springs. Take Old Hwy 80, 2 mi. to the Boulder Oaks Cpg. and access to the Pacific Crest Trail. Walk under the highway bridge, then stay right after the bridge, climbing steeply into the Cleveland National Forest. A little less than 2 mi. At 3,910 ft. look for a trail that goes north into Kitchen Creek. At the creek walk 100 yds downhill to find shallow basins at between 3,400 and 3,600 ft.

Spur Trail

32° 44' 09"N
116° 27' 39"W

Kitchen Creek

32° 44' 35"N
116° 27' 53"W

Map Source: DeLorme Topo3.0

Kitchen Creek

Forget the falls. (Which for some reason aren't shown on the topo anyway.) The aesthetic is at the basins and tubs above the cascade where everything appears as if in miniature—all beautiful in a diminutive way. Wildflowers, sedges and even grass make the pools at the top more enchanting than the fall itself which runs 150 feet over polished slabs into steep, fast tubs which are not safe for swimming. The tubs up on top, though, are perfectly crafted for blowing bubbles on a hot day or doing a water ouzel impression. Hikers on the PCT might use the creek for a fast soak, but, hidden as it is 200 yards below the trail, it seems to escape a lot of traffic. Also it's a little tricky finding the spur trail then scrambling the last 100 vertical feet over some loose rock.

The best time to visit is in April. The watershed is only about 20 square miles, so it dries up pretty quickly. Also, the ceanothus and manzanita are in bloom and light breezes are redolent with honey and spice. Be prepared to share the trail with bees.

There's some steep climbing—900 vertical feet in two miles to reach the spur trail. Then minor bushwhacking to an inconsequential scramble leading to the basins. Running shoes should be more than adequate.

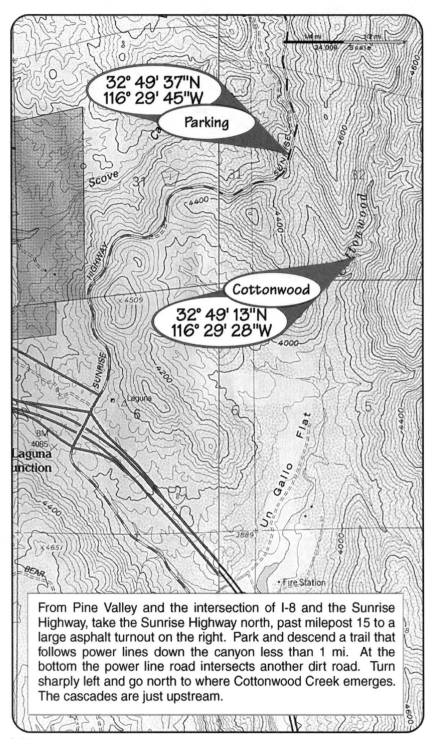

32° 49' 37"N
116° 29' 45"W

Parking

Cottonwood

32° 49' 13"N
116° 29' 28"W

From Pine Valley and the intersection of I-8 and the Sunrise Highway, take the Sunrise Highway north, past milepost 15 to a large asphalt turnout on the right. Park and descend a trail that follows power lines down the canyon less than 1 mi. At the bottom the power line road intersects another dirt road. Turn sharply left and go north to where Cottonwood Creek emerges. The cascades are just upstream.

Cottonwood Creek

It's hard to stay put at Cottonwood Creek Falls. All the twists and turns in the creek keep drawing you farther upstream. Several sharp turns make this stream seem something like a labyrinth and each turn is followed by a small fall with a tub or small basin below. Hardly grand enough to make *National Geographic,* but it is a nice place. The stream bed is composed of a rock laid down on the same angle as the water flow, giving the stream something of a paved look. The drainage faces south, producing sweltering temperatures during the summer. A shallow basin in the middle is deeply shaded by trees, but water there will become stagnant earlier in the season.

There are more than 70 miles of hiking trails in the Laguna Mountains. This isn't one of them. Access from the roadside turnout is via a brushy draw draining south. After a few hundred yards of moderate bushwhacking you pick up an old road that follows some power lines. That road intersects another heading north up the canyon.

The brushy descent aside, Cottonwood Creek is easy enough to get to that it's a good place for families. Pick a hot day in spring when the water level is still up and before the moss gets long and shaggy. There are some good-looking oak trees just below the falls that make a nice place for a family picnic.

Why Bother

Sill Hill Waterfall
An attractive puddle.

Maidenhair Falls
Little more than a shower. Not swimmable.

Upper Hellhole Canyon
Devil to get to. Not a lot of water.

South Fork Sheep Canyon
Anza Borrego desert. Key word here is desert. Short season, if any.

Lower Cougar Canyon
Ditto.

I n d e x